THE BEST DAYS OF MY LIFE

Scharada Dubey is an award-winning author of books for children and adults. She won the First Prize in the Commonwealth Essay Competition in 1973 and second place in the Outlook-Picador Non-Fiction Competition in 2000. She has also won several prizes for her children's books. Her earlier books include *Icons of Social Change* and *The Hanuman Heart*.

Scharada lives and works in Faizabad, Uttar Pradesh.

REMEMBER THE DAYS WE SPENT TOGETHER AS CHILDREN AT "ST JOHNS WOOD" ALWAYS.

WILL MISS U

Isha

← ME TOO
- ISHA

Lots of Love
Samar & Saheena
31.3.2011

The Best Days of My Life

Childhood Stories of Famous People

Scharada Dubey

Portraits by Zainab Tambawalla

SCHOLASTIC
New York Toronto London Auckland
Sydney New Delhi Hong Kong

Text © 2008 Scharada Dubey
Illustrations © 2008 Scholastic India Pvt. Ltd.
All rights reserved.

Published by Scholastic India Pvt. Ltd.
A subsidiary of Scholastic Inc., New York, 10012 (USA).
Publishers since 1920, with international operations in
Canada, Australia, New Zealand, the United Kingdom,
India, and Hong Kong.

No part of this publication may be reproduced in whole or in
part, or stored in a retrieval system, or transmitted in any form
or by any means, electronic, mechanical, photocopying,
recording, or otherwise without the written permission of the
publisher.

For information regarding permission, write to:
Scholastic India Pvt. Ltd.
Golf View Corporate Tower-A, 3rd Floor,
DLF Phase V, Gurgaon 122002 (India)

Typeset in Bodoni MT by Mantra Virtual Services, New Delhi

First edition: June 2008
Reprint August; November 2008
May; September 2009; June; July; September 2010

ISBN-13: 978-81-8477-014-8

Printed at Vimal Offset, Delhi

Contents

Gautama Buddha

(BC 563 – BC 483)

Siddhartha Gautama or Gautama Buddha is known all over the world as the great teacher who taught human beings the way out of suffering. His message found acceptance in ancient India and across the world and led to the evolution of what we know as Buddhism. As the first person to have opened the way to enlightenment for all human beings, he is considered to be the Supreme Buddha by Buddhists. Gautama Buddha is also known as Shakyamuni, or 'sage of the Shakyas' because he was born a prince in the Shakya dynasty. Buddha renounced royal life at the age of twenty-nine. After encountering an old crippled man, a sick man, and a decaying corpse, he decided to seek an answer to the problem of birth, old age, sickness, and death. He attained enlightenment and spent the remaining forty-five years of his life teaching his disciples and followers how to lead life according to the doctrine of the Middle Path, avoiding the extremes of both, excessive self-indulgence and severe asceticism. Buddhism spread throughout Asia, but it has gained a wide following in the Western world only in modern times. Buddhist values of peace, mindfulness and care for all living creatures are particularly relevant to us in the face of today's challenges of violence, terrorism and unchecked materialism.

The princes walked in a leisurely and erratic fashion through the forest glade. Stopping to sip from a stream, or to discuss a spectacular bloom or fruit, they walked slowly, accompanied by a few attendants. Devadutta marched ahead, using a stick in sword-like fashion to swish away the vines and plants that came in their path. Siddhartha was quiet and contemplative, drinking in the wild beauty of the forest and its inhabitants.

They reached a lake, and found a cluster of swans on its mirrored surface. As they paused to take in the sight, Devadutta reached instinctively for his bow and arrow. The swans began to circle the lake. One of them took off in graceful flight and the others followed. Thrilled and excited by the sight, Devadutta raised his bow and took careful aim. He shot an arrow at the birds in flight. However, he did not know whether the arrow had found its mark.

Meanwhile, Siddhartha had walked on ahead. A little way down the forest path, he noticed the mute form of an injured bird. Stooping to the ground, he picked up the swan whose body had been pierced by Devadutta's arrow. The bird was bleeding, its heart beating with fright and pain. It seemed almost dead. However, Siddhartha pulled out the arrow from the bird's body and tenderly laid the bird on a bed of grass. He stayed the bleeding with an application of green leaves. Under his concerned and caring gaze, the bird slowly began to revive.

When Devadutta caught up with them, he asked

his cousin to hand him the swan, claiming the bird as his own. Siddhartha refused to part with the bird. 'The bird is mine because it was I who shot him down,' said Devadutta, panting with anger and exertion. His cousin fixed him with a firm and clear look. 'Well, if the bird is to be claimed then it is mine, because I gave it a chance to live.' So saying, he lifted the bird up with both hands, and set it free. Miraculously, the swan which had seemed to be struggling for breath only moments earlier, flapped its wings a few times and flew away in graceful flight, emitting a small sound, perhaps of gratitude to its liberator.

A furious Devadutta vowed to take up the matter with the palace elders, but he knew it was no use trying to convince his cousin any more. Siddhartha was calm and composed, but he was clearly the victor of this particular encounter.

Siddhartha was born in Lumbini and grew up as a prince in Kapilvastu, both of which are in modern-day Nepal. His father King Shuddhodana was the chief of the Shakyas, one of several ancient tribes in the growing state of Kosala. His mother Queen Mahamaya had a strange dream on the night Siddhartha was conceived. She reported having dreamt of a white elephant with six white tusks entering the right side of her body. On her way to her father's kingdom for the delivery, the queen gave birth to Siddhartha at Lumbini, in a garden beneath a sal tree.

Unfortunately for the infant, Siddhartha's mother

died seven days after giving birth to him. He was named Siddhartha, meaning 'one who achieves his aim', and brought up by his mother's sister, whom king Shuddhodana married after his mother's death. His birth was an event of great celebration and on the fifth day after his birth, the hermit seer Asita predicted that the child would either become a great king or a great holy man. Asita made this prediction by examining the birthmarks on the soles of the baby's feet. To his consternation, King Shuddhodana found this prophecy repeated by eight other Brahmin scholars whom he invited to read his son's future. One scholar, Kaundinya, disagreed with the duality of this prediction. In his opinion, there was no doubt—the young prince would grow up to be a great holy man and teacher.

Shuddhodana drew strength from the either/or nature of the prophecy about his son. He hoped that he could avert one part of the prediction and see to it that his son became a great king. Determined to shield his son from the influences that could turn him towards a spiritual search, he brought him up in the lap of luxury, building three separate palaces for him to occupy at different times of the year. He was also kept away from religious books, and anything that could prompt him to question human existence and suffering.

The boy who should never have been concerned about anything but his own pleasure was, however, a deeply sensitive individual. From the time he was a child, Siddhartha felt the experience of all forms of life as his own. He also achieved meditative states that were quite uncommon in a child, or even in a mature adult. This form of spontaneous meditation once happened on a festive annual occasion when the king, like any common man, ploughed the fields himself. A feast followed this ceremonious occasion. As the people assembled at the feast, Siddhartha wandered off quietly by himself until he came to a nice, shady apple tree. He slipped spontaneously into a state of meditation that made him feel one with all living beings. At the same time, he saw a chain of events. A lizard darted out its tongue, licking up and eating ants. Then a snake came along and swallowed the lizard. Before long, an agile hawk swooped down on the snake. The prince saw and understood that life is change, and all creatures possess something that is beautiful and not beautiful at the same time.

When Siddhartha reached the age of sixteen, his father arranged his marriage to his cousin Yashodhara, wanting him to become involved in the responsibilities of family life. After a few years, Yashodhara gave birth to a son, Rahul. Although Siddhartha left behind this family when he renounced his royal existence at the age of twenty-nine, Yashodhara was not against his spiritual journey and search. In fact, with her encouragement, Rahul later joined the other disciples of Gautama Buddha, the teacher of the entire world.

Kabir

(1440 – 1518)

Kabir is undoubtedly one of the greatest poets and mystic saints ever born in India. Through his life and poetry, he taught that all human beings are equal, all life represents interaction between God on the one hand, and the individual human soul on the other, and true salvation lies in achieving the union of both. Kabir's dohas contain social criticism as well as a rejection of religious hypocrisies like excessive austerity, rituals, chanting and other practices. Kabir's poems brim over with love for God, even as he asserts that both God and guru (teacher) can be known through direct experience. Kabir lived among the people, a humble weaver and an ordinary human being, completely aware of his connection to God at every moment. What makes Kabir especially important is that his work and teachings represent a synthesis of Hindu and Muslim ideas. While he believed in the Hindu concept of reincarnation and the law of karma, he also followed the practices of Indian Sufi ascetics derived from Islam. In fact, Kabir's poems have not only influenced Muslims and Hindus but people of all faiths. Over five hundred of his poems were collected by the fifth Sikh guru, Guru Arjan Dev, and form a section of the *Guru Granth Sahib*, the scripture of the Sikhs.

Two poor Muslim weavers, Niru and his wife Nimma, were walking around the Lahara Tala lake near the holy city of Varanasi. The couple had no children. As they made their way along the shore, Nimma cried out in surprise, 'Look, there's a baby floating on that lotus leaf!'

'Hush!' said her husband. 'You long so much for a child that you have started imagining one wherever you go!'

'No, no, look!' said Nimma agitatedly. 'The little baby is flailing its arms and legs. Please save the child from falling in the water!'

When Niru looked in the direction in which his wife was pointing, he saw that there was indeed a tiny infant floating on a large lotus leaf in a bed of water lilies. Wading into the water of the lake immediately, he came back carrying a small boy. Amazingly, this abandoned infant, instead of crying loudly as any ordinary child would have done, looked up into the faces of his rescuers and smiled a sweet, toothless smile.

'Praise be to Allah!' exclaimed Nimma. 'Is this beautiful gift really for us? How can I ever thank God enough for showering me with such joy?'

The overjoyed couple took the little baby home and brought him up as their son. They named him Kabir— one of the ninety-nine names of Allah found in the Koran, meaning the greatest one. The local people speculated that the child must be the son of a Hindu brahmin widow, who had abandoned the baby, not knowing how to care for it. But for Niru and Nimma, where Kabir came from was not as important as the joy he had brought into their lives. He was a happy, lovable boy who seemed to radiate a kind and loving spirit towards those he met.

Kabir showed an intense curiosity towards religious and spiritual matters from a very young age. He also showed an understanding and intelligence far beyond his years. Even though he learnt how to weave from his father, and played with ordinary children from the village where he lived, it was clear that he was special.

One of the ways in which he was different from the other children was his desire for a guru who would help him progress on the spiritual path. A famed saint named Ramanand, who was a disciple of the great Vaishnavite seer Sri Ramanuja from South India, was the person Kabir most wanted as his teacher. But how would a Hindu saint accept a Muslim child as his disciple? No one knew how Kabir would find a way out of this seemingly impossible situation.

In the Hindu annual calendar there is a day on which anyone can become a disciple by having a master speak the name of God over him. Knowing that Ramanand went to bathe in the Ganga before dawn like all the other ascetics living in Varanasi, Kabir lay in wait for him on the steps of the bathing ghat. Returning from his dip in the river in the pre-dawn light, Ramanand unwittingly stepped on the body of the young boy who lay barring his path. Shocked and sorry for inadvertently causing hurt, Ramanand exclaimed aloud, 'Rama! Rama!' At this, the boy jumped up in joy, then prostrated and touched the guru's feet. 'You have spoken the name of God over me, dear master!' he said. 'Now surely, you will have me as your disciple!'

Looking down at the eager face of the young boy, Ramanand saw that 'Kabir' in Arabic lettering was tattooed on the back of the boy's hand. He immediately realised that the boy had been raised in a Muslim household. However, impressed by Kabir's intelligence and intense desire to take up religious training, Ramanand accepted him as his disciple. Even though his arrival in Ramanand's ashram created a stir, and some Hindu students even left in protest, the saint was not affected. He preached the equality of all human beings, and students of several different castes were his students.

As for his young student, he was destined to make people of different religions think more deeply about the common objective of their respective faiths, rather than harp on their differences. While not much is known about what sort of spiritual training Kabir may have received from Ramanand, he was encouraged to grow into an adult life much like his father's. He did not become a sadhu, and went on to marry and have children. He lived the simple life of a weaver, yet possessed the inner knowledge of a great mystic. In fact, he is said to have attained enlightenment while he was in Ramanand's care. What is more remarkable is that Ramanand's own enlightenment, or sense of complete oneness with God, is said to have come after Kabir's!

As Kabir began to spread the message of love and union with God, his followers began to appear among both religions—Hinduism and Islam. He wrote his poems in a Hindi dialect that was clearly understood by the common man. He urged those around him to abandon the scriptures and instead concentrate on leading a simple and natural life. This approach to enlightenment began to be known as the *Sahaj* (or natural) path. For Kabir, training in Hindu Vedantic concepts did not mean embracing orthodoxy, but living by the actual Vedanta philosophy of spurning the caste system and idol worship. Kabir emphasised the concept of a *nirguna* or formless God, who was at once everywhere, in each one of us, and nowhere, because He could not be confined to any one spot. This made Kabir close to the Bhakts (other devotional poets and mystics that emerged in different parts of India) as well as the Sufis (followers of the mystic tradition in Islam).

Kabir's unconventional approach challenged both the religious orthodoxy as well as the authority of rulers who supported social discrimination. After he was banished from Varanasi at the age of sixty, he lived the wandering life of an exile at many places in North India, with a group of his followers. He died at Maghar, near Gorakhpur, in 1518.

Even today Kabir's life and work inspire us to end religious hatred and spread the message of universal love. While a student of Kabir may have to make an attempt to understand the dialect and vocabulary of the past, he or she will be rewarded with insights about being human and being at peace with God. Kabir's knowledge, wisdom and love reach out across time to those who seek him.

Leonardo da Vinci

(1452 – 1519)

Leonardo da Vinci is known variously as an Italian painter, sculptor, architect, musician, engineer and scientist. This is because his versatile intelligence was applied to the observation and study of many things—from the anatomy of human beings, animals, birds and plants, to the devising of mechanical objects that later became universally known, such as the paddle boat, the robot, or even the umbrella. Deriving his name from Vinci, a hill village in Tuscany, near where he was born, Leonardo da Vinci is the foremost example of Renaissance genius and artistry. His drawings depict flying machines with scientific precision, many centuries before they came into existence. From his notebooks that have inspired many designers and artists since his time, we can get a good idea of the range and depth of one of the greatest minds humankind has produced. He is best remembered as the painter who painted the famous *Mona Lisa* and *The Last Supper*.

A kite swooped down from the sky and fell onto the lap of the child lying peacefully in a large wooden cradle. Caterina had left the baby Leonardo sleeping in the cradle out-of-doors while she worked in the fields. Frightened and disoriented by its fall, the large bird, with its curved predatory beak, flapped its wings against the soft clothes and pillows swaddling the infant. As it beat its wings in panic, its feathers struck the infant's mouth. Too stunned to cry at first, the baby set up a wail after the bird had freed itself and flown away. But while he cried, he could still recall how the feathers of the bird had felt against his lips.

This traumatic incident may have gone unnoticed if the baby had not grown up to be one of the greatest inventors, designers and artists the world has ever known. Perhaps it was because of this early childhood encounter with the fierce-looking kite that Leonardo da Vinci developed a great curiosity for birds and the mechanism of flight! He would later draw diagrams for building flying machines in great detail.

Leonardo was born in Anchiano, a village near Vinci, Italy on April 15, 1452. He was the son of Ser Piero d'Antonio, a young notary and Caterina, a peasant girl who may have worked as a barmaid. Because he was born out of wedlock, he spent the first few years of his life with his mother in the village. His father had left for Florence soon after his birth and was a busy young lawyer there. He had also been convinced by his family to settle down with a woman from a very wealthy family. Caterina, meanwhile, had been quickly married off to a cowherd from a village named Accattabriga. They soon had many children.

With his mother distracted by her other children, and his father busy in Florence, Leonardo lived a few years with his paternal grandparents. After some years, however, it was discovered that his father's wife could not have children. It was then that his father Ser Piero took Leonardo to the city to be raised and educated in his father's house.

In these years, Leonardo moved from one home to another, and although he received affection, he never got the undivided attention of a parent. Left to his own devices, Leonardo grew up with a lively curiosity about the world around him. He was especially attracted to nature, and recorded the habits of animals and birds. In a way, his being an outsider or an illegitimate child freed him from the burden of having to follow in anyone's footsteps. During this time, his father's brother, Francesco, encouraged him to pursue drawing, because no one expected him to become a notary.

He spent a lot of time with his uncle Francesco, tending to animals and roaming around farmland, fully absorbing the landscape that he would later sketch and study. Thus Leonardo developed his great appetite for knowledge, becoming the universal man that exemplified the time in which he lived—the European Renaissance. This was also a period when human understanding was being freed from the clutches of oppressive rulers and stifling religious beliefs. Leonardo da Vinci could choose to study anything he wanted, and record his observations with the fine, unerring eye of the true artist.

From as long as he could remember, Leonardo loved to draw. Once, while exploring the mountains, he chanced upon a cave that went deep into the hillside. He later spoke of his emotions at this discovery, as being on the one hand, terror at some great monster lurking inside, and on the other, curiosity to find out what was inside. This curiosity that helped him overcome ordinary fear is what set him apart in his quest for knowledge. While his father provided him with the tutors who gave him an elementary education, Leonardo learnt many things on his own, such as establishing a lifelong practice of self-study that would lead him to later master Latin, physics and human anatomy.

After being accepted into his father's home, Leonardo began to live in the city, but he retained contact with his mother right up to his adult years, and was thus able to gain from his observations of both the country and its people, and the city and its modern ways. As a young child in his father's home, Leonardo's extraordinary talent emerged in different ways. He was able to achieve a high level of proficiency in music with astonishing speed, when he learnt to play the lyre. He also learnt to sing, and those who heard him were touched by his pure and beautiful voice. He was extremely good at mathematics—this was, in fact, the foundation on which he would build his later studies of physics and mechanical design. In the city, he continued to sketch all that caught his attention.

When he was thirteen years old, his father, recognising his marked aptitude for drawing and art, sent him to study with the most sought-after Florentine artist of that time, Andrea Verrocchio. Verocchio was a renowned sculptor, painter and goldsmith. Leonardo now had the opportunity to learn the techniques and methods associated with different arts, such as grinding and mixing colour pigments for painting, mastering geometry and learning the proportions and perspectives that are so important in art. He was also responsible for preparing panels for placing paintings, and had ample opportunity to observe closely the actual act of painting, and the working of clay and bronze casting that is integral to sculpture. While not too much has survived of Verocchio's own work, he is today more famous as the master who taught Leonardo da Vinci his first techniques.

In 1472, at the age of twenty, Leonardo enrolled as a master in the company of painters. Professionals banded under associations called guilds in that period, and if Leonardo was proficient enough to be accepted as a master, it indicates that his actual apprenticeship to Verrocchio had ended by this time, though he continued to stay on at his master's workshop.

While Leonardo da Vinci may be best known throughout the world as the painter of the *Mona Lisa*, he actually did far more drawing than painting as an artist. He drew copiously in large notebooks, keeping extensive notes alongside that explained facets of the drawings. Few paintings may have survived the onslaught of time, but Leonardo's precious notebooks, filled with his drawings of people, places and things have been found in various parts of the world and over 10,000 drawings have been recovered. *The Vitruvian Man*, a drawing that is a study of the anatomy of a man, has become a classical symbol of the human body over centuries. One of the strange aspects of da Vinci's notebooks is that the detailed notes by da Vinci were sometimes in code, or in the intriguing form of letters written backwards—mirror writing, a form of writing that apparently came easily to this most accomplished genius!

It is these cryptic features that have led to renewed curiosity about Leonardo da Vinci's work in the present day, through immensely popular books like *The Da Vinci Code* by Dan Brown.

Abraham Lincoln

(1809 – 1865)

Abraham Lincoln was the sixteenth president of the United States. He ranks among the top three presidents the US has ever had, because in his short time in office Lincoln did more to build the American nation, than any other president before or after him. The foundation for true equality between all American citizens was laid by the firm convictions and actions of Lincoln. Frederick Douglass, a man who was born a slave but went on to become a famous orator, statesman and reformer described Lincoln's actions as 'essential to Negro freedom.' Abraham Lincoln's measures to abolish slavery—the practice of employing people from African countries as labour in the fields and homes of white American settlers—and his leadership during the American Civil War have earned him a lasting place in the history of his country.

It was only a small fish, but the boy who was carrying it home for dinner was proud of his catch. For a four-year-old, it was a great feeling to have caught a fish on his own. He looked forward to showing his catch to his mother.

As little Abraham walked on the path through the woods around Knob Creek, a man in a soldier's uniform approached him. As he came near the boy, he paused to greet him and enquired, with a kind twinkle in his eyes, 'Good day, young man! Did you catch that fine fish all by yourself?'

The child nodded, noting the soldier's travel-weary clothes. The soldier looked as if he had been on the road for some days. After a few minutes of conversation, the boy remembered his family's advice to 'be good to soldiers'. Holding out the only thing he had to offer in the nature of a gift, he said, 'Would you like this fish for your dinner?' The soldier, hungry and grateful for the generosity of this small child, accepted the offering with a smile of thanks.

Neither the child, nor the soldier who accepted his gift knew then that the little boy would grow up to be one of the finest and best-loved presidents of the United States of America.

Growing up as a child in a family of pioneers—men and women who made their way into the wilderness to open it up and make way for others to follow—Abraham Lincoln became used to being among the trees and streams of the forest at a very early age.

Abraham's father, Thomas Lincoln, was a wandering labourer who had learnt carpentry. He could neither read nor write. It was only after he got married that his wife, Nancy Hanks, taught him how to sign his name.

Abraham Lincoln was born in a log cabin on Rock Spring Farm which his father, Thomas, had brought on credit. His family lived there for the next four years. They later moved to a better and bigger farm in Knob Creek, a short distance away, where they lived till he was seven.

Spending long hours on his own meant that Abraham created imaginary friends and foes for himself as he roamed the forest. Abraham also gained in physical strength, learning to climb, run swiftly, leap over long distances, and carry heavy branches home for firewood.

His first brush with education was through a tutor named Zachariah Riney, who taught a small group of children from the pioneers' families near the Lincoln cabin. The next teacher was Caleb Hazel, whom they had to travel four miles to meet. There was sometimes a gap of weeks and even months between one set of lessons and the next.

In the autumn of 1816, when Abraham was just seven and his sister Sarah nine, Thomas Lincoln decided to move with his family to a forest near Pigeon Creek.

The family made the journey over several nights and days. They arrived to set up their home in a heavily wooded spot. It was already late autumn, and they had to build a shelter as soon as possible against the approaching frost. Thomas Lincoln used his carpentry skills to quickly put up a camp. He later began work on a cabin.

Seven-year-old Abraham helped his father with all

the heavy work involved in making the cabin. An unusually large and strong child, he learned early how to wield the axe. Many years later, after becoming president, he recalled that an axe 'was put into his hands at once', and from that time till his twenty-third year he was almost constantly handling it. Abraham travelled seven miles on horseback to a nearby settlement to grind a bag of corn at a hand grist-mill so his family could make bread.

Two years later Abraham's mother died of a mysterious illness. Abraham's sister, Sarah, was only eleven years old, and struggled to cope with household tasks. The small family carried on for some time under this deadly blow. Then in the autumn of 1819, Thomas Lincoln married Sarah Bush Johnston, a widow from Kentucky.

Not only was Abraham's new stepmother responsible for bringing material comforts into his home, she also encouraged Abraham to study and improve his talents.

From a schoolhouse of round logs, and split log benches, with Webster's *Elementary Spelling* Book as the only textbook, Abraham Lincoln began his journey in search of knowledge! In the Pigeon Creek settlement, books, slates, pens, ink or paper were luxuries.

By the time Abraham was able to go to school again, he was fourteen, then seventeen. Despite the long gap between one period of instruction and the next, Abraham learned to write.

Under such trying circumstances it would have been only too easy to forget about an education altogether. But Abraham was exceptional in his desire to learn. Every spare moment was spent in some kind of study. He had a copy book that served as a kind of scrap book of all the passages he had read and liked. He did sums on the fire shovel, the broad, wooden oar-like instrument whose one end narrowed to a handle. Working on this wooden shovel by the flickering firelight, he would use his drawing knife to shave the shovel clean when it had been covered with his charcoal writing.

Abraham borrowed books as often as he could in order to improve his reading and knowledge. *Robinson Crusoe*, *Aesop's Fables*, *Pilgrim's Progress*, the *Life of Washington*, and a *History of the United States* formed the substance of his reading in these years. But it was not reading alone that occupied him. He also worked on his father's farm, and assisted neighbours who needed a helping hand.

Abraham Lincoln grew up much like other boys around him on the pioneering frontier except for one major difference. The one sport in which Abraham never joined his mates was hunting.

While boys of his age took early to the rifle, and hunted the wild creatures in the forests around them for food and fur, Abraham abstained from hunting altogether. The time that his peers spent lying in wait for their quarry, he spent in reading and learning. His gentle nature clearly shrank from hurting or injuring other living creatures. This gentle, generous and determined lad grew to shape his country's destiny like few have done before or since.

Swami Vivekananda

(1863 – 1902)

Swami Vivekananda is one of the most influential and outstanding spiritual leaders the world has ever seen. It was his dream to put India on the path of greatness by inspiring every Indian to fulfill his or her potential. He was the chief disciple of Ramakrishna Paramahansa and founded the Ramakrishna Math and Ramakrishna Mission after his guru's demise. Swami Vivekananda's powerful oratory first focused the attention of the West on the spiritual heritage of India, when he addressed the Conference of World Religions in Chicago in 1893. A complete patriot whose life was dedicated to the welfare of the country, Vivekananda sought to impart the values that would lead to the progress of the poor, the helpless and the downtrodden. His brilliance, determination and spirit of sacrifice were something India badly needed at the end of the nineteenth century and beginning of the twentieth, when years of British rule had created a sense of inferiority in the people. Vivekananda's inspiring words and writing remain to remind us that we need have no fear, and can be masters of our own destiny.

The schoolboy looked boldly into the eyes of his teacher. A stunned silence had descended upon the class. 'Naren, what you say is wrong,' insisted the geography teacher. 'No, Sir, it is right,' answered the boy, continuing the confrontation.

'I am telling you, it is not in the book. If it is as you say, then shouldn't it be in the textbook?' questioned the teacher.

'Yes, sir, it should be there in the textbook, and it is,' said the boy. ‹

'Don't argue with me!' the teacher exclaimed loudly. 'For this argument alone I shall beat you black and blue!' So saying, he picked up a cane and began to beat the boy. Thwack! Smack! The angry sound of the cane made the other children in the class wince in pain. But the boy on whom the blows were being rained remained unmoved and unrepentant. Putting down the cane with shaking hands, the teacher finally went to open the textbook to verify the boy's claim. To his intense shame, he found that the boy had been perfectly right.

When his mother rushed to greet Narendra on his arrival from school, she was shocked to see the marks of the cane on her son's hands and back. 'What happened, son?' she asked in anguish. The boy narrated to her the incident with his teacher, wondering if he was to receive another scolding. But when his mother had heard him out, she looked far from unhappy. In fact, she was smiling as she patted his head and blessed him. 'I am really happy and proud of you, my son,' she said. 'Whatever the odds you will never be found to swerve from the path of truth.'

The boy who faced the teacher's unfair wrath was Narendranath Dutta. He was born on January 12, 1863, in Calcutta. His father was a famous lawyer named Vishwanath Dutta. Well-educated and widely travelled, Vishwanath Dutta believed in scientific study and modern liberal thought. He spoke several languages, including Persian and English. Narendra's mother, Bhuvaneswari Devi, was a deeply spiritual person who inculcated the values of fearlessness, honesty, justice and determination in her son. She narrated stories from the Ramayana and Mahabharata to Narendra. Hers was undoubtedly a very important and formative influence on a boy who later became famous the world over as Swami Vivekananda.

However, this is not to say that the boy was especially pious or religious in his childhood. In fact, Narendra had a very lively and enquiring mind, and was as naughty as the other children he played with. The only difference was his complete absence of fear, and his exceptional honesty. Young Narendra was occasionally very restless as a result of boredom with his immediate environment. He also had a very bad temper for one so young. It was his dauntless spirit, and his love and trust for his mother that made him fearlessly confess all his childish pranks to her.

His parents searched for ways to contain the restlessness that Narendra exhibited from an early age.

They tried to channelise some of his restless energy into subjects like music and art. Narendra studied vocal music, as well as played the *pakhwaj*, a percussion instrument. He also appeared to be extremely intelligent. Just a glance at a printed page of his schoolbooks and he had the entire content mastered almost as though he had memorised it!

Narendra's extraordinary ability to tap into his own immense inner potential was best demonstrated by his ability to meditate. He could enter deep meditation at the age of eight, apparently quite effortlessly and easily. Even as a young boy, Narendra questioned the validity of superstitious customs and discrimination based on caste and religion. He would ask questions of his elders that ridiculed such practices, insisting on a more egalitarian and just view of reality. On the other hand, he also respected sanyasis or ascetics right from when he was a child. He was always willing to give anything to anybody. A beggar just had to ask him for something, and Narendra would give him what he had. Such a spirit of sacrifice and renunciation marked Narendra's childhood.

During his growing-up years, several people noticed his exceptional abilities and prophesied his greatness. As a teenager, he would openly doubt the existence of God, and would question those who seemed to be more spiritually advanced about their experience of the divine force. Once he had questioned Maharshi Devendranath, the father of Rabindranath Tagore with such determined thoroughness that the elder had tried and failed to answer the questions of the bold adolescent. Looking into the sceptical face of Narendra, Maharshi Devendranath declared, 'You possess the eyes of a yogi.'

Another important instruction that led to the formation of Narendranath's adult personality was the advice given to him by his worldly-wise father when he was in high school. 'To show surprise at anything amounts to a tacit expression of ignorance, and hence of weakness. Never show surprise,' Vishwanath Dutta told his son. In later years, it would seem that the boy had absorbed this advice really well—he met people drawn from all sections of society, from the poorest to the richest, and his eyes never revealed surprise at the striking differences he observed in the world. However, while his father's lack of surprise probably denoted a worldly self-control, in Narendra's case it was the deeper, all-encompassing acceptance of a true sage.

Narendra was only eighteen when he encountered the master who would define the remaining days of his life—Sri Ramakrishna Paramahamsa. When Narendra passed out of school he had completely mastered Western logic, western philosophy and history. At this time, he was briefly associated with the Brahmo Samaj, an important religious movement of the time, led by Keshab Chandra Sen. Narendra wished to satisfy his own doubts regarding the existence of God. But the prayer meetings and devotional songs of the Brahmo Samaj alone could not satisfy Narendra's curiosity.

On a casual visit to Dakshineswar with his friends, Narendra met Sri Ramakrishna, a priest in the temple of Kali. This simple priest had no pretensions of being a scholar, but he was sought by all as a great devotee of the goddess. When Narendra met him, he asked, 'Have you seen God?' The instantaneous answer he received from Ramakrishna, 'Yes, I have seen God, just as I see you here, only in a more clear sense,' startled him. Completely convinced about the honesty of this man's words, that seemed to have come out of deep experience, Narendra started visiting Sri Ramakrishna frequently.

Their association presented the world with an outstanding example of humanitarianism and devotion.

Marie Curie

(1867 – 1934)

Nearly two hundred and fifty years after she was born, Marie Curie is still the best-known woman scientist, even in the twenty-first century. Born in Poland, she moved to France at the age of twenty-four, and subsequently took up French citizenship. Her life showed complete dedication to the cause of science, even in the midst of trying personal tragedies. Her name will always be associated with the field of radioactivity. The first person to receive a Nobel Prize on two different occasions and for two different sciences, Marie Curie was awarded the Nobel for physics in 1903 and for chemistry in 1911. She was also a pioneer in terms of being the first female professor at the Sorbonne in Paris. She founded the Curie Institutes in Paris and Warsaw. Remarkably, she was the wife of fellow Nobel laureate, Pierre Curie, and her daughter, Irène Joliot-Curie, became the third Nobel laureate in their family.

The Sklodowska family studied together in the evenings, so that the parents who were both teachers could help the children, Zosia, Bronya, Hela and Jozio with their homework. Wladyshaw Sklodowski had a huge appetite for learning and made sure his children grew up with a respect for education. His wife, Bronislawa was the headmistress at a girl's school in Warsaw, Poland.

One evening, as her seven-year-old sister Bronya stumbled over a passage she had to read aloud, Wladyshaw and Bronislawa's youngest child, little three- and-a-half-year-old Marie, or Manya, as she was called at home, picked up her older sister's book. Taking up from the point where Bronya had left off, she began reading fluently, effortlessly, from the textbook, completely unaware of the astonished expressions of her family members. When she looked up and saw the almost horrified look on the faces of her parents and siblings, she grew frightened and burst into tears. 'I did not do that on purpose!' she said, explaining her action. 'It was just so easy!'

This incident was typical of the young girl who would later grow up to be a world-famous scientist in physics and chemistry. She was extremely intelligent, but she was also very sensitive, and felt events with a keenness that would stay with her all through her life.

In her childhood, Marie looked up to her father, as did all the Sklodowska children, considering him a walking encyclopedia because of his vast knowledge of many different subjects. His father, Marie's grandfather. Jozef Sklodowski, had also been a teacher and a school principal who had sought to end social inequality by encouraging children of peasant families to study in the same class as the children of the landed gentry.

When Marie was born on November 7, 1867, in a town house on Warsaw's Freta Street, her mother was the headmistress of one of Warsaw's better girls' schools, adjoining their home. For the first few years, Marie, who was the youngest of five children would see her mother struggling with the work of running a big household as well as the school. In these years, the house had visiting guests, as well as students, and one of these, Wladyshaw's brother, came to live with them when he was ill, in the terminal stages of tuberculosis. This disease, which spreads mainly through the germ-infected air when somebody who already has the disease coughs or sneezes, afflicted Marie's mother when Marie was still quite small. The disease was then incurable, managed by a series of rest and recuperation treatments in places where the climate was not so cold. Thus began a period of yearning for little Marie because her mother often had to be away at a sanatorium in the south of France. Only Marie's oldest sister, Zosia, could go with her.

Even when Bronislawa was at home, she was extremely worried about her children contracting the disease from her. She often lay isolated in a separate room away from the children. The greatest gesture of love she permitted herself was gently patting their heads. She tried to compensate for the lack of physical demonstrativeness by playing the piano and singing for them, or reading and telling them stories. For Manya, her youngest child, heaven meant those moments when she lay down by her mother's feet, closed her eyes and listened to her sing.

The illness meant that Mrs Sklodowska could not go back to teach, and the family began to feel the financial pinch from this loss of income. They began renting rooms out to students, and Marie's mother, who had brought her children up not to regard work done with their hands to be in any way inferior to 'brain work', hit upon another method of saving money by sewing the shoes for her children to wear.

The greatest tragedy of young Marie's life occurred when her mother died a few months before her eleventh birthday. Afterwards, Marie and her sisters would often play a make-believe game about a genius doctor who finds a miracle cure for a serious illness. Marie's dream of using science and medicine to help humanity was rooted in her encounter with tragedy very early in life. Not only did she lose her mother, but two years before this tragic event, her elder sister Zosia had passed away, too.

The foundation of Marie's later learning was laid in her childhood by her father's diligent efforts to teach his children Greek, Latin, Russian, Polish, French, German and English by reading to them, besides sharing with them books on physics and chemistry. Marie took so naturally to learning and reading that her parents tried to prevent her premature development by distracting her with outings and boisterous games.

46

However, every time she found a quiet moment, Marie would return once more to the books and become totally absorbed. Once, to tease her out of her reverie, her sisters and brother piled up some furniture behind her back as she read, and then brought it down with a loud clatter. Marie did not turn a hair, or even look around, but when they drew her attention with loud hoots of laughter, she declared, 'That's silly!'

During her childhood, Poland was occupied by Russian forces. When she began studying in the private school of Miss Sikorska, there were periodic inspections by Russian inspectors to see if the children were being taught Russian. It was forbidden to teach the children in their own mother tongue of Polish, but the teachers did just that. Marie's teacher, Antonine Tupalska, knew Marie's flawless grasp of anything that was taught to her. When the inspectors arrived to check the students' knowledge of the Russian language and history, Marie Sklodowska was always put forward as the example to be interrogated by the inspector. She spoke flawless Russian and answered all the questions put to her, but the effort sometimes proved to be too great a strain on Marie. After each such ordeal, Marie would weep in the arms of Miss Tupalska, her nerves exhausted by the effort of covering up for the whole school.

After her mother and eldest sister's deaths, it had been Marie's sister Bronya who had taken over the responsibility of looking after the family. And yet, Bronya managed to complete her schooling by being the topmost student of the school. As her sister, Marie felt an intense pressure to do similarly well, and applied herself in the last five years of school to studying really hard. When she graduated from school at the age of fifteen, she earned herself a gold medal as the best student. However, her father could see the effect of this intense effort on Marie's health and decided to send Marie and her other sister Helena to spend a year on the country estate of their wealthy uncle and aunt. Here, for the first time, Marie relished the outdoor life, riding, fishing, swinging dangerously on swings and rowing a boat on a lake. Winter gave them the opportunity to go on sleigh rides through the snowy Polish countryside and they also enjoyed dancing the night away at manor house parties. During this period, Marie met famous Polish artists and intellectuals who dropped in at her uncle's place, giving her a much-needed glimpse of the world of ideas, arts and science. For an earnest young girl whose short life till then had been marred by so much pain, this was a wonderful period that helped restore her spirit and prepared her for the momentous future that lay ahead.

Mahatma Gandhi

(1869 – 1948)

Mohandas Karamchand Gandhi, known across the world as Mahatma Gandhi, is widely acknowledged as the most influential political and spiritual leader of the Indian independence movement. He taught us the power of Satyagraha— a means of resistance to unjust laws and practices through mass civil disobedience, based on total non-violence. This has inspired movements for civil rights and freedom in many countries since the struggle for Indian independence. Affectionately called 'Bapu' or father, in his lifetime, Mahatma Gandhi has officially been accorded the honour of being called the Father of the Nation. The UN General Assembly has unanimously declared October 2, his birthday, as the International Day of Non-Violence. Gandhiji's childhood and formative years have been described by him as experiments with truth, and right and wrong, that helped him develop a strongly moral and determined character. It was this strong character that led the Indian community's struggle for civil rights in South Africa, and the nationwide campaigns for the alleviation of poverty, for the liberation of women, for unity and fellowship among differing religions and communities, for an end to untouchability and caste discrimination, for the economic self-sufficiency of the nation, and above all for Swaraj—

India's freedom from foreign rule. It was Mahatma Gandhi's call to make the British 'Quit India' in 1942 that mobilised the entire nation. In his years of struggle, Gandhiji was imprisoned for many years on numerous occasions in both South Africa and India. He was finally felled by an assassin's bullet on January 30, 1948.

The story of Harishchandra, the king who stood by the truth in all circumstances, is a powerful episode in Hindu mythology. A play based on the story of this king was being enacted before a small-town audience. A young boy was among the people who were watching the drama unfold, showing King Harishchandra suffering and losing his kingdom for refusing to abandon the truth, but no one could have imagined the deep effect the scenes were having on the young boy's mind and heart.

'I will never swerve from the path of truth, and be ever-truthful and honest like Harishchandra,' thought the boy to himself.

This quiet, intensely shy and sensitive boy was called Mohandas Karamchand Gandhi. Born on October 2, 1869, in Porbandar on the Saurashtra coast, he was the youngest son of Karamchand Gandhi , the diwan or prime minister of Porbandar, and his wife Putlibai. When Mohandas was seven years old, his family moved east to Rajkot. This was the place where he spent his childhood, although the family retained the link with Porbandar.

In Rajkot, little Mohandas avoided all company. He was so anxious to avoid any unnecessary social encounters that he always rushed to school on time and rushed back home as soon as the school bell rang, afraid of talking to anyone on the way. Not only that, he was also afraid of the dark, ghosts, thieves, snakes and many other things. This excessive timidity once made Rambha, a maid at his home, ask him in exasperation, 'Why are you so frightened? What are you afraid of? Remember Rama! He will always protect you. He who remembers God need never be afraid of anything!'

These words were to have a powerful effect on the timid young boy, who began to pray to Rama with all his heart whenever he was afraid. Thus was laid the foundation of a whole life of unshakeable faith. As a boy, it was his mother's whole-hearted love and strong will power that was the most enduring example to Mohandas. She lived an austere life, and made him move towards mastering his own selfish and lesser impulses. Perhaps it was the abundant love she showered on him that led to his later being able to embrace all of humanity.

While from her influence he imbibed the Jain influences of Gujarat, such as the tenets of non-injury to living beings, vegetarianism, fasting for self-purification, and mutual tolerance between members of various creeds and sects, his marriage at the tender age of thirteen to Kasturba taught him the power of silent resistance. Kasturba was quiet and determined, and when Mohandas tried to bend her to his will, he found that she resisted in a non-violent but very resolute fashion.

Many years later, Gandhiji recalled in an interview what he had learned from Kasturba. 'Her determined resistance to my will ... and her quiet submission to the suffering my stupidity involved ... ultimately made me ashamed of myself and cured me of ... thinking that I was born to rule over her, and in the end she became my teacher in non-violence.'

Mohandas' perception of the truth evolved out of many incidents that are quite common to many young boys and girls. What was distinct about him was his ability to learn an important lesson after each experience. He had a passion to always tell the truth. When the inspector of schools came to visit his school, he dictated a few English words to the boys to test them. Seeing that Mohandas could not spell one of the words correctly, his teacher signalled that he could copy that word from his neighbour's slate. But Mohandas sat stubbornly still. He could not cheat, even under the urging of a teacher. All the students except him got all their spellings right. For his refusal to copy, Mohandas got scolded by the teacher after the class. He was deeply hurt, but in the end, satisfied for having done what he knew was right.

The more dramatic incidents relating to his awareness of the truth and how to choose right over wrong concern his temporary lapse from the vegetarianism practised by his family, and one occasion when he stole a piece of gold from his brother's bracelet in order to have money to buy cigarettes for smoking. On both these occasions, Mohandas learnt important lessons about the value of truthfulness.

With India being under British rule, people speculated in all manner of ways about the source of British power and strength. A friend once told Mohandas, 'The British are so strong and can rule over us because they eat meat! How can we fight them if we stay vegetarians? If we become meat-eaters, like them, we will be able to drive them out.'

Mohandas was convinced by this statement, but as his family was strictly vegetarian, he had to take up eating meat outside, in a clandestine manner. However, when he realised that the meat-eating was actually pushing him into a position of lying to his family, he decided never to do it again. Mohandas was more concerned that he should not become morally weak by getting into the habit of lying even if it was at the cost of becoming physically very strong.

Another time, a friend convinced him to try smoking the cigarette butts they both found lying around, and this led to both of them developing a taste for the habit. To buy cigarettes, Mohandas stole money and went into debt. When the debt became too much to bear, he paid it off with a piece of gold stolen from one of the gold bracelets that his brother wore.

There was no respite for Mohandas after that. He could not sleep, or be at peace, tormented by the thought of his crime. As he analysed why he had reached such an abject state, he resolved never to steal again. Writing a truthful account of all he had done, he put the piece of paper into the hands of his ailing father.

His father read the letter and, instead of an angry punishment, what Mohandas got was a deep sigh from his father, who tore up the paper without saying a word. For the sensitive boy who had always resolved to be wedded to the truth, this sign of disappointment was more of a punishment than a hundred angry words. Mohandas was full of remorse for his actions. He wept aloud, and served his sick father in every way he could. The whole experience had only strengthened, forever, his commitment to the truth.

Mahatma Gandhi's greatness did not lie in his never

doing wrong. It lay in his learning from each experience of wrong, and staying with what was right and good, through whatever difficulties he had to endure.

Albert Einstein

(1879 – 1955)

Albert Einstein is widely regarded as the greatest physicist of all time. He contributed enormously to our understanding of natural phenomena and the way things work. His exceptional genius has made him a symbol of superhuman intelligence in the popular imagination. Einstein put forth many theoretical observations, of which some of the most memorable are the photoelectric law in which he discussed the behaviour of light. This knowledge laid the foundation for the development of television and motion pictures with sound. He explored the relation of mass to energy with the famous equation $E=mc^2$, which was used to develop atomic energy and the hydrogen bomb. His Special Theory of Relativity applied mechanics to principles of electromagnetism. In 1921, Einstein was awarded the Nobel Prize in physics for his services to theoretical physics. Although the theory he expounded was used to develop the atomic bomb, Einstein despised war, and is famous for saying, 'Science without religion is lame, religion without science is blind' as he sought to build a balance between scientific enquiry and spiritual wisdom.

Dressed in formal clothes, the five-year-old boy waited on a sofa in the living room for his parents to get ready. He was accompanying them to a dinner party. The little boy kept looking at an object clutched in his hand. No matter which way he turned the object, the movable needle inside the object always pointed to the north. As he waited, the boy continued to experiment, squinting into the small glass surface of the compass his father had given him as a gift.

'What is this invisible force that pushes the needle to point to the North?' wondered the child. As he gazed at the pocket compass, he was sure there was something behind things, something deeply hidden, and he was determined to find out what it was.

Albert Einstein was born on March 14, 1879 in Ulm, Germany. His father, Hermann, was an electrical engineer. His mother, Pauline, was a musician. When Albert was a year old, his family moved to Munich, where his father started a company that made electrical equipment and lighting. The little boy was quiet, self-sufficient and quite remarkable. Although he did not seem unhappy, and was quick to understand things, he did not attempt to speak, like other children. By the time he was two, he was still maintaining a dignified silence, rare in a child who was not born with speech impairment.

Then one day when he was three years old, he startled his family at the dinner table by uttering a complete sentence, 'My soup is too hot.' His stunned parents stopped eating, and all conversation was abandoned as everyone turned to gaze at him. 'You spoke so wonderfully!' cried his mother. 'Did you know how to do that all along?' Albert nodded. 'Then why didn't you speak, son?' asked his father. 'You know, we have been so anxious about your silence.' To which the little boy answered in explanation, with great composure, 'Everything has been fine.'

Albert had a problem with speech through his growing years. He would take time to answer questions, slowly mouthing the words before saying them aloud. But his intelligence was obviously focused on a very active inner world—a place where his imagination roamed free, attempting to solve the mysteries of life.

On his mother's insistence, young Albert took violin lessons. Although, like many children, he disliked this regimen and tried to avoid classes whenever possible, he later developed a life-long passion for music, particularly the violin sonatas by Mozart. But more than musical talent, Albert began to show a great talent for mathematics, which was nurtured by his Uncle Jakob. This jocular uncle introduced Albert to algebra, calling it a 'merry science' because it made one hunt a little animal called 'x'! Only when the sum had been solved could one find out what the animal was. Uncle Jakob gave Albert books of algebra and geometry, and made learning fun for him by using examples from everyday life. Many years later, the adult Albert followed a similar model in his teaching, by using trains, elevators and ships to explain theories to his students.

Albert Einstein was born to Jewish parents, but studied in a school where all the children were Catholics. Because of his slow and deliberate manner of speaking, and his generally dreamy appearance, his teachers despaired of him ever doing anything well. Oblivious to this bleak vision of his future, the little boy began to build models and mechanical devices as a hobby. The one absorbing hobby that showed his capability to concentrate on a single goal for hours on end was building a house of cards!

In spite of the attitude of his teachers, there was no dearth of adults who encouraged his talents. Apart from Uncle Jakob, a struggling young medical student named Max Talmey who was a friend of Albert's family and shared a meal with them every week, encouraged Albert's exploration of maths and science. He introduced key science and philosophy texts, such as Kant's *Critique of Pure Reason* and Euclid's *Elements* to the ten-year-old Albert. It was through Euclid's book, that he later called the 'holy little geometry book', that Albert began to understand how to think in ways integral to theoretical physics. It was because of these early inputs that he could learn Euclidean geometry from a school booklet by the time he was twelve. Soon thereafter, he was ready to investigate calculus, the most abstract of all mathematical sciences.

Small wonder then that with so much going on outside of school hours, Albert was bored with the more sedate curriculum of school at the Luitpold Gymnasium, the Catholic school he attended. In 1894, when Albert was fifteen, his family moved to Milan in Italy, but Albert had not yet finished school and his parents wanted him to complete the school year in Munich. But Albert was not interested in staying back in Munich. He wanted to be in the warmer and more comfortable climate of Italy with his family. He convinced a doctor to give him a certificate stating that he had a lung condition that needed him to move to a drier climate such as the one where his parents were living. He then used his persuasive powers on the school authorities to give him a certificate in mathematics for direct admission into college. The school administration actually gave this great genius such a certificate because they wanted to get rid of him!

With the intention of applying directly to the Swiss Federal Institute of Technology in Zurich, Albert Einstein attempted an entrance examination, but did not pass. He then spent a year at a school in Aarau where he had the good fortune of having excellent teachers and first-rate facilities in physics, his favourite subject. It is a measure of his calibre as a scientist that his first important scientific paper was written when he was only fifteen, that too in the midst of the many changes that were occurring in his life. This work was titled 'The Investigation of the State of Aether in Magnetic Fields'. The following year, even though he failed the entrance examination for the institute at

Zurich, he conducted his famous thought experiment, in which he visualised travelling alongside a beam of light. This remarkable thought travel by a sixteen-year-old, was to revolutionise science and technology in unimaginable ways. Einstein can truly be said to have been light years ahead of his time.

Ironically, though Einstein had nothing to do with the invention of the atomic bomb, it was his discovery of the power of atoms that actually led to the discovery of the bomb. Before World War II broke out, Einstein had been living in America for some years. On August 2, 1939, he and some fellow scientists, wrote a letter to the then-president, Franklin D. Roosevelt, alerting him about the efforts in Nazi Germany to purify uranium, and the likelihood of its being used to build an atomic bomb. Soon after this, the US government put into place the Manhattan Project, which was committed to the research and production of an atomic bomb. When the first bombs were used to bomb Hiroshima and Nagasaki in Japan on August 6 and August 9, 1945, Einstein was saddened and distressed. Haunted by the thought that he had been a catalyst in the making of the bombs, Albert Einstein called his signing of the letter to President Roosevelt, the 'one great mistake in my life …' just a few months before his death.

Helen Keller

(1880 – 1968)

Helen Adams Keller was an American author, activist and lecturer, who even years after her death is an inspiration to the disabled all over the world to overcome their physical handicaps and lead full and active lives. Born as a normal child, she became deaf and blind as a result of an illness at the age of nineteen months. The illness also affected the development of her speech, leaving her severely disabled. A remarkable teacher called Anne Sullivan helped Helen not only break through her isolation, but also become the first deaf-blind person to graduate from college. After completing her education, Helen Keller became a radical campaigner for workers' rights and spoke out against child labour and capital punishment. Her most inspiring book is *The Story of My Life*. In addition to this, she also wrote eleven other books, as well as articles on blindness, deafness, social issues and women's rights. She met several famous and distinguished people throughout her life, who admired her courage and determination. Helen Keller received many honours, among them the Gold Medal of the National Institute of Social Sciences in 1952, an honour by the Sorbonne in Paris in 1953, and the United States' highest civilian honour, the Presidential Medal of Freedom, in 1964.

The well stood in the garden at a small distance from the main house. The path leading to it smelt strongly of honeysuckle—the flowering vine that covered the roof and sides of the well house. The deaf and blind girl walked along the path to the well, holding her teacher's hand. When they reached, someone was drawing water from the well with a hand-pump. The teacher drew her pupil's hand and put it under the water spout, letting the cool stream of the water flow over the girl's hand.

Then gently holding the girl's other hand, the teacher pressed her finger into the child's palm and spelt the word 'water'. A simple enough gesture, but it unlocked a whole world of perception and understanding in her sensitive and intelligent student. This little girl, who had seemed to be so severely handicapped that she was beyond comprehending speech and language, went on to learn thirty new words that same afternoon. The teacher and her pupil had discovered a way to overcome seemingly insurmountable limitations.

This miraculous afternoon of April 5, 1887, was the turning point in little Helen Keller's relationship with her teacher, Anne Sullivan. It represented the beginning of her triumph over disability that would spell hope for millions of people in times to come.

Helen Keller was the daughter of Captain Arthur Henley Keller and Kate Adams Keller. She was born on June 27, 1880 in Tuscumbia, a small rural town in Northwest Alabama in the US. Helen had perfectly sound sight and hearing at birth. Her father had been a captain in the Confederate Army during the American Civil War, but by the time of her birth, her parents were struggling to maintain their station. They lived in a house built by Helen's grandfather, and Captain Keller worked at two jobs—that of a cotton farmer and as editor of a local paper called the *North Alabamian.*

Life for the small family would have been tranquil had it not been for Helen contracting an illness—either scarlet fever or meningitis—when she was just eighteen months old. When she recovered from this severe illness, her parents' relief turned to horror on discovering that she had lost both sight and hearing

Now began a period of extreme tribulation. Little Helen turned into a terror and a tormentor, as she fought hard to come to terms with a soundless, sightless world. Looking wild and unkempt, Helen became a very difficult child whom many relatives regarded as being fit only to be put into an institution. Completely unable to communicate or comprehend anything her family was trying to tell her, Helen screamed and banged her head in frustration, threw things in her rage, snatched food from people's plates, and refused to have her hair combed.

Her desperate family sought help, and a Baltimore doctor directed them to an expert on the problems of deaf children—Alexander Graham Bell, more famous as the inventor of the telephone. Bell put them in touch with Michael Anagnos, director of the Perkins Institution and Massachusetts Asylum for the Blind, whom they requested to find a teacher for Helen. Anagnos had no hesitation in recommending a former pupil of his institution, Anne Sullivan.

When Anne Sullivan arrived at Helen's home, she had been through her share of hardship. She had lost a large part of her sight by the age of five, her mother had died when she was just ten and she had been abandoned by her father. She and her brother Jimmie were packed off to an orphanage in 1876, where her brother died. Anne could leave the orphanage and begin her studies at the Perkins Institution only in 1880. While she was studying at Perkins, two operations on her eyes led to her regaining enough sight to be able to read a little for short periods of time.

After graduating from Perkins, Anne had been struggling in search of work and so although she had no experience in this area, she jumped at the chance to work as the teacher of Helen Keller, a hearing-vision- and speech-impaired student.

Helen Keller believed that her life really began on March 3, 1887, the day Anne arrived at Helen's house in Tuscumbia and met her for the first time. She had brought a doll as a present for her pupil, and as she pressed the present into her hand, she also tried to write 'doll' on Helen's other palm. She did the same with other objects like 'cake'. Helen repeated the finger movements, but she could not understand what they meant. Anne not only struggled to help her understand, she also worked hard to control Helen's rising anger and tantrums.

Anne and Helen were housed in a small cottage in the compound of the main house to continue Helen's education. When Anne tried to make Helen brush her hair or button her clothes and shoes, Helen responded with huge tantrums. Anne had to control these tantrums by refusing to spell words on Helen's hands— their only form of communication.

However, their daily interactions formed a definite bond between teacher and pupil, and people began to notice an improvement in Helen's behaviour. Anne had been teaching Helen for barely a month before the day of the 'miracle' when she learned the word 'water'. Quite unsurprisingly, one of the first words Helen asked to learn after this, on that same afternoon, was 'teacher'.

From then on, Helen made remarkable progress, and her ability to learn was truly exceptional, considering her double handicap. Anne first taught Helen to read with raised letters, then with braille, and to write with both ordinary and braille typewriters.

Michael Anagnos was quick to note this triumph, and he began to promote Helen through articles in the press. Soon, pictures of Helen reading Shakespeare or stroking her dog began appearing in national newspapers, and the eight-year-old was suddenly famous. Helen's fame led to her visiting President Cleveland at the White House.

In 1890, she began living at the Perkins Institute where Anne continued to teach her. She also began trying to learn to speak under the training of Mary Swift

Lamson. However, this proved unsuccessful, and Helen was able to master a limited range of sounds that only Anne and others very close to her could understand.

When she graduated with honours from the prestigious Radcliffe College in 1904, Helen Keller was showing the way for innumerable others to conquer their own limitations. But this victory could never have been achieved without Anne Sullivan, the teacher with whom she shared a lifelong partnership.

Jawaharlal Nehru

(1889 – 1964)

Jawaharlal Nehru was a major participant in the struggle for Indian independence, and later went on to become the first prime minister of independent India. A staunch nationalist who worked for social reform, he was born into a wealthy family and was educated in England. Nehru is considered by many to be the architect of modern India, and is recognised across the world as a statesman who championed the cause of world peace. Jawaharlal Nehru was elected president of the Indian National Congress five times and it was under him that the Congress adopted the famous resolution of complete independence at its Lahore session in 1929. During his prime ministership, India made rapid technical and industrial advances and achieved self-sufficiency in key areas. He also initiated India's nonalignment policy in foreign affairs, ensuring India's autonomy in a world dominated by two superpowers. A skilled orator and writer, Nehru is known for his 'Freedom at Midnight' speech and his books which include *Glimpses of World History* and *Discovery of India*. Because he loved children so much and spent many happy hours in their midst, November 14, his birthday, is celebrated as Children's Day across the country.

The large house with a sizeable garden in the city of scholarship and pilgrimage—Allahabad—provided the backdrop for the young boy's imagination. Here, roaming the gardens or visiting the stables where the family horses were housed, Jawaharlal, son of Motilal Nehru, was virtually alone for the first eleven years of his life.

His three sisters were much younger than him, so a series of English governesses and tutors were the main sources of instruction for the boy who got used to his own company. Although he was extremely polite and well-behaved, he did not develop an attachment for any of these teachers, apart from Ferdinand Brooks, who made a lasting impression on him. Jawaharlal's upbringing was very much in the tradition of the West—in manners, dress and language—but he was also provided a grounding in the culture of his country by a special tutor who taught him Hindi and Sanskrit.

Books took the place of siblings or playmates and Jawaharlal developed an interest in the leading authors of the time, including Walter Scott, Charles Dickens, Thackeray, H.G. Wells and Mark Twain, as well as philosophical and political writers like John Stuart Mill, Gladstone, John Morley, Bertrand Russell and Bernard Shaw. Later in life, his fluent speech and powerful articulation would draw the attention of world leaders. Doubtless, the books he read in childhood contributed towards making him an orator and author.

Motilal Nehru was a famous barrister based in

Allahabad, whose Kashmiri brahmin family had moved there from Kashmir a few generations earlier. A patriot who was a member of the Indian National Congress, Motilal was married to Swaroop Rani. Their first child, Jawahar, was born on November 14, 1889. While Motilal's intense involvement with the Congress meant that Jawaharlal was exposed to discussion and debate about India's independence from a very early age, father and son differed in their approach in later years. Motilal, like several others in the Congress leadership, was ready for India to be given dominion status within the British empire, on the other hand Jawaharlal, fired by the ideals and principles of Mahatma Gandhi, was committed to fighting for total independence.

The influence of Ferdinand Brooks, who was a Theosophist, awakened an interest in the society of spiritual seekers in the young Jawaharlal. He joined the Theosophical Society at the age of thirteen. This connection would find continued expression in 1917, when the young man, now trained as a lawyer, would protest the imprisonment of Annie Besant, an Irish Theosophist who had committed herself to the cause of India's freedom. It was this issue that drew Jawaharlal into the Home Rule League, marking the beginning of his political career.

The privilege and prestige accorded to the very rich marked Jawaharlal's childhood, and he was sent off to England to study at the age of fifteen. This departure marked a long period in which he would attend first, school at Harrow, and then, university at Cambridge, finally studying to become a barrister at the Inner Temple in London. In 1912, Jawaharlal Nehru returned to India, and began practising law at the Allahabad High Court.

During his long stay in England, Jawaharlal did not display any exceptional degree of scholarship. In fact, this period was pleasant and enjoyable because Jawaharlal could indulge in some of the usual activities of a fashionable young English gentleman. He spent time playing tennis and rowing, and even indulged in some mild forms of gambling. His shyness proved to be something of a handicap in these years—when he was on the Cambridge debating team, he often had to pay fines for not speaking during the entire term!

From such a privileged and problem-free existence, Jawaharlal Nehru was catapulted into the rough and tumble of Indian politics by a series of events that led to his awakening. Apart from the issue of Annie Besant's imprisonment in 1917, the most stirring changes in Jawaharlal's consciousness happened in 1919, the year of the Jallianwalla Bagh massacre, when 400 Indians were shot at the order of a British officer, and in 1920, when he first encountered at very close quarters, the extreme poverty of millions of his countrymen.

Jawaharlal first met Mahatma Gandhi in 1919. He was struck by how Gandhi, in spite of having had an education quite similar to Nehru's, remained essentially Indian in everything he did. The relationship between the two would shape all Jawaharlal's future thinking and actions. The year 1920 was a further milestone in Jawaharlal's discovery of his own Indianness. On a rural tour where he met peasants and villagers, Jawaharlal was 'filled with shame and sorrow ... at the degradation and overwhelming poverty of India.' This moving experience strengthened his commitment to fight for the poorest and most disadvantaged. While he had embraced Fabian Socialism as an idea in his student days in England, his socialism would become much more firmly grounded in the face of real-life conditions in India. He attempted to organise the peasants. It was from this time that Jawaharlal began to be primarily Indian in lifestyle, approach and expression. He read daily from the *Bhagavad Gita*, and practised yoga. He began to dress in the Indian clothes of *kurta*, *sherwani* and *churidar*, with the cap that would become a distinguishing feature and the inspiration for Congress men thereafter.

In 1916, Jawaharlal's marriage was arranged with Kamala Kaul, a young Kashmiri woman brought up in an orthodox Kashmiri brahmin family. Their daughter Indira Priyadarshini was born in November 1917. When Jawaharlal adopted the Indian style of dress and speech, and began following Mahatma Gandhi's values of simple living, his wife gladly adopted them too. Their daughter was brought up in an environment completely dominated by India's struggle for independence.

Jawaharlal, who had described himself while at

Cambridge as, 'In my likes and dislikes I was perhaps more an Englishman than an Indian' evolved into a towering figure of the Indian freedom struggle and a leader of independent India who gave shape to her identity on the global stage.

Enid Blyton

(1897 – 1968)

Enid Blyton was one of the most popular and prolific authors of children's books in English. In a forty-year writing span, she wrote more than 700 books that have been translated into nearly 70 languages, and have sold over 400 million copies throughout the world. Some of her stories, aimed at young readers, featured pixies and elves, goblins and fairies, or the characters of the world of toys, as in the Noddy series. But among her adventure and mystery books for older children, the most famous series is of The Famous Five characters Julian, Dick, Anne, George, and their dog Timmy. Teamwork, courage, honesty, and a lively curiosity about the environment besides elaborate descriptions of good food are the hallmarks of her books. While she has the distinction of having introduced whole generations of young readers to the pleasures of books, her writing became a source of controversy in multi-racial Britain in the 1980s as some of the content was considered sexist, racist and outdated. But the sheer popularity of her books outlived the controversy, proving how successfully she has been able to ignite the imagination of millions of children.

'Oh Enid, have you been sitting with your nose in a book the whole time I've been gone?' said Theresa despairingly to her daughter as she pulled off her gloves and put away her hat. It was a winter evening and the shadows had lengthened all around the house. But Enid had been so absorbed in reading that she had forgotten to lay the table for dinner, or put away the laundry, or even light any lamps other than the one she was reading by. Theresa's mouth tightened in disapproval of her daughter. Enid was the eldest of her three children.

Jumping up at the sound of her mother's voice, Enid said, 'Heavens! Are you back? Is it time for dinner? I'm sorry, I didn't realise it was late. Hanley and Carey have hardly made a sound!'

'Fat chance of you even noticing if they had,' said her mother grimly, continuing to look disapprovingly at her daughter, whom she considered too much of a bookworm and not enough of a help in housekeeping.

Enid was already rushing about trying to make up for lost time doing the things she had been meant to do. If she noticed the strongly disapproving tone of her mother, she tried not to let it get her down. 'She'll calm down,' Enid was thinking. 'And it's not wrong for me to want to play, or read, or write tons and tons of stories if I want to. Papa understands, and he says it's okay.'

This self-belief in the face of family disapproval was very necessary for the development of a writer who went on to delight millions of readers with her real and heart-warming descriptions of childhood. If Enid had toed the line and done only the household chores, instead of living in her own fantasy world, fed by books, the world would have been much the poorer!

Enid Blyton was born on August 11, 1897, in a small flat above a shop in Lordship Lane, East Dulwich, London. Her parents were Thomas Carey and Theresa Blyton, and she was their first child. Her father worked for a cutlery firm. He had grown up in Sheffield and had later moved to London. Though he had a mundane job, he was a man of many interests who enjoyed reading, and had developed many hobbies. Enid inherited his love of books and the outdoors.

As a young girl, some of her most enjoyable moments were spent with her father, walking for hours in the countryside, where he passed on to her his knowledge of nature and wildlife, and they discussed the books beloved to them both. Compared to this, her relationship with her mother always had an undercurrent of tension.

After a couple of years in London with the young Enid, her parents moved to Chaffinch Road in Beckenham, Kent. Here, Enid's brother Hanley arrived in 1899. Later, in 1902, their third sibling, a brother named Carey, was born. When Enid's father began working for a clothes firm with a better salary, they moved to a big house on Clockhouse Road in Beckenham with a big garden. Enid and her brothers played a lot in this garden, and gardens and houses play an important role in her stories and books. In fact, many of her stories actually describe a house she inhabited later in life, called Green Hedges.

At one point in her childhood, she was stricken by a particularly severe bout of whooping cough, so threatening in its effects that her parents thought she would die. Typically, she describes the children recovering from this ailment in one of her Famous Five books, making fun of the way their coughs sound!

Enid fairly devoured books, especially books like *Alice in Wonderland*, so intriguing for children in those days, with its enigmatic characters and imaginary world. However, her passion extended to outdoor activities too, and she enjoyed sports. According to some biographers, the character of George, the hot-tempered tomboyish girl of the Famous Five series, was based on herself. No doubt, there must have been a little bit of Enid in all the stories she wrote, stories that have enthralled children for decades. For instance, in the Naughtiest Girl series, a girl joins boarding school, behaves atrociously in the beginning, but leaves the school as its head girl. From 1907 to 1915 Enid was educated at St Christopher's School in Beckenham, where she did well in studies and sports, and became the head girl.

Enid's growing years were affected by the marital strain in her parents' relationship. In 1910, things between her mother and father had taken a turn for the worse, leading to him moving out of the house. This departure must have been undoubtedly traumatic for Enid, particularly because of the close bond she shared with her father. Her father kept in touch with the family, and provided some support to her mother in bringing up the children, but the comfortable years of the family being together were gone forever.

They now moved to a less comfortable house in a slightly downmarket area of Beckenham. In her teens, Enid wrote stories and poems prolifically, determined to have them published, but her initial attempts met with a lot of rejection. Her first published work was a poem published by Arthur Mee in a magazine in 1911. She had been having piano lessons for several years, and showed some aptitude for music. Her father's family had its share of musical talent, and it was believed that Enid would follow this vocation. However, she astonished her family when she refused to take the music any further. She was determined to pursue her writing, and as a further departure from music, she began training to become a teacher.

Undoubtedly, it was Enid Blyton's intimate knowledge of what makes children happy, what fascinates or repels them, and what makes them stand by each other that gave her such an edge as an enduringly popular children's author. This knowledge was acquired not only during the long private hours Enid Blyton spent as a child, reading and creating her own private universe, it was also built up over the years as Enid interacted with children, as a teacher, as a mother, and as an author.

J.R.D. Tata

(1904 – 1993)

Jehangir Ratanji Dadabhoy Tata was an industrialist and the pioneer of civil aviation in India. In 1929, he was given the first pilot license issued in India. Three years later, in 1932, he founded India's first commercial airline, then called Tata Airlines, which became Air India in 1946. It has been India's national airline ever since. Coming from a family of industrialists, JRD, as he was called by most people, held a position of leadership in the Tata group of companies, with their considerable interests across many industrial segments. Companies like Tata Steel (or TISCO), TELCO, the Taj Group of hotels, Tata Consultancy Services and others, have been household names for decades in independent India. J.R.D. Tata contributed to the growth of all these. In his long career, JRD set high ethical standards in business, refusing to succumb to corruption and bribery. He was also famous for his contributions to several distinguished institutions of higher education. Awarded the Padma Vibhushan in 1957, he was decorated with the Bharat Ratna in 1992 for his service to industry and nation building. A man who was loved and respected by anyone who came in contact with him, J.R.D. Tata was mourned by millions when he passed away in 1993, at the age of eighty-nine.

This was a treat far greater than what the fifteen-year-old could have imagined. For years, his famous neighbour, the great aviator, Louis Bleriot, had fascinated him. As a child, JRD remembered the headlines which proclaimed Bleriot's pioneering flight across the English Channel in an aircraft, in 1909.

Now this same neighbour was inviting him to go up in a plane with him! For the boy who loved planes and everything associated with flying, this first flight was thrilling beyond measure. He savoured the sensation of soaring above green fields and country homes, conquering an element still new and inviting for human enterprise—the blue sky.

On that flight in the French countryside with his distinguished neighbour, Jehangir Ratanji Dadabhoy Tata, or Jeh as he was called, found his resolve to become a pilot grow stronger than ever.

J.R.D. Tata was the son of Ratanji Dadabhoy Tata and his French wife Sooni (Suzanne Briere before her marriage). Ratanji was a cousin and colleague of Jamshetji Tata, the pioneer who founded the Tata group of companies in India and is credited by many as having brought the industrial revolution to India. Ratanji and Sooni's family divided their time between Bombay and Paris at the beginning of the twentieth century. On July 29, 1904, their second child, a son, was born in Paris. He was the second of five children. The boy was named Jehangir, a Persian name signifying conqueror of the world.

Growing up in France, JRD spoke French, his mother's language, better than any language he learnt subsequently. The family faced a fair bit of disruption because of the widespread nature of Ratanji's business interests. They spent some years in Yokohama in Japan, besides France and India; JRD's school education was thus often interrupted. However, his mother Sooni was a very intelligent and adaptable lady. It was her resourcefulness that helped her to single-handedly pack up her household belongings and move along with her five children from France to India and Japan to be with her husband. She went back to her own country every year or two on long visits, accompanied by her children.

JRD was thus close to his French family, particularly his grandparents. As he described them to his biographer R.M. Lala, his grandmother was a formidable lady who inspired awe in most people. About his grandfather, JRD said, 'Her husband was a humorist and after some time with her, the gentleman ran away as anyone would have, had he been married to my grandmother.' This observation about the figures from his childhood shows JRD's own humorous nature.

A childhood incident JRD recalled was the sound thrashing he received from his father when he was four, for being rude to his *aayah* or nurse. While this curbed any tendency to be rude for his entire life, it also spoke of the firm values taught to JRD and his siblings by their parents. The children may have led a privileged life, surrounded by comforts and being served by others, but they were taught never to abuse or disgrace such a privileged position. 'You cannot be rude and show disrespect towards anyone, no matter who they are' is the clear message that stayed with JRD, and in fact, it was clearly reflected in his dealings with others. He had a quick temper, but showed unfailing courtesy and respect towards all he met.

On his father's side, JRD's family was of Persian-Zoroastrian descent, part of the Parsi community who had first arrived on the Gujarat coast when they came to India some time between 716 and 936 AD. The community showed remarkable enterprise and had a high degree of education, and Jamshetji Tata, JRD's father's cousin, was the most renowned entrepreneur-industrialist among this distinguished lot. While JRD's early years may have been mainly spent in France, the growth of industry in India, led by Jamshetji's vision and enterprise, formed a good part of his heritage. He spent some years studying at Cathedral and John Connon School in Mumbai. He also attended school in Japan. Finally, because his English needed to improve so that he could attend university at Cambridge in England, JRD was sent to an English grammar school to master the language.

Cambridge was not to figure in JRD's education, however. He would be educated in the much larger and more challenging school of life itself. After school, he was drafted for a year into the French army as part of compulsory military service and was assigned to the

Regimente de Spahis. At the end of the mandatory year, the army still held sufficient romance for the youthful JRD to want to continue serving in the regiment. Besides, if he continued military service, he would be able to go to a premier horse-riding academy attended by army officers. This prospect beckoned JRD, who was passionate about horses and riding. But his father had other plans. He called JRD to India to join the Tata companies as an apprentice learning the ropes, and so not only halted his army career, but also cancelled his plans to go to Cambridge.

While giving up his dream to study engineering at Cambridge must have seemed particularly disappointing to the young JRD, one incident vindicated his father's stand. Soon after JRD had left the Regimente de Spahis, the entire regiment was wiped out while on an expedition to Morocco. As for his lack of engineering education, JRD's vision and skills would give direction to hundreds of talented engineers who shaped India's industry and created many valuable products.

JRD had first joined the Tatas as an unpaid apprentice in December 1925, when he was just nineteen. Three years later, soon after his father passed away, JRD joined the board of Tata Sons, the flagship company of the Tata Group. In 1929, at the age of twenty-five, he surrendered his French citizenship, became an Indian citizen and got his pilot's license. He became the fourth chairman of the Tata Group in 1938.

Some guiding principles of JRD reflect the nature

of his remarkable personality and his deepest convictions.

'One must forever strive for excellence, or even perfection, in any task however small, and never be satisfied with the second best.

'No success or achievement in material terms is worthwhile unless it serves the needs or interests of the country and its people and is achieved by fair and honest means.

'Good human relations not only bring great personal rewards but also are essential to the success of any enterprise.'

Tenzing Norgay

(1914 – 1986)

Tenzing Norgay was a Sherpa born in Eastern Tibet who later lived in Nepal and India. He is most famous for the first conquest of the world's tallest mountain, Mount Everest, on May 29, 1953. Tenzing became a professional mountaineer and climbed up to Everest's summit many times during the twenty years following his and Edmund Hillary's first successful climb. He later worked as director of field training for the Himalayan Mountaineering Institute in Darjeeling, and set up his own company in 1978 to provide trekking help and guidance in the Himalayas. Tenzing died of a bronchial illness in Darjeeling in 1986. He became a legend in his lifetime, and earned himself a place alongside world leaders who admired his courage and simplicity. He was an inspiration not only for other mountaineers and Sherpas, but also for the lay public. Known by many titles such as 'Man of Everest' and 'Tiger of the Snows' by his admirers, Tenzing remained a friend of his fellow climber Edmund Hillary. This long association helped bring recognition for the unique mountaineering skills of the Sherpas, and an appreciation for their culture with its innate respect and reverence for the mountains and the environment.

'If you stare too long at Chomolungma, your yaks will get away from you!' the elders passing the boy on the mountain passes would jocularly tell young Tenzing. A somewhat serious and quiet boy, his habit of day-dreaming while keeping his gaze fixed on the distant peak of Mount Everest, had become common knowledge among the people of the hills.

Tenzing walked the mountain paths of the Kharta Valley with his yaks. This valley lies in the shadow of the earth's tallest mountain, and from the time that he could remember, Tenzing had always had Chomolungma, as the Tibetans call Everest, as his reference point on the horizon. The people among whom Tenzing lived had a deep reverence for Chomolungma. They considered the mountain home to Miyo Lungsangma, the mother goddess of earth. Tenzing imbibed the values of family and community during his life in the mountains. It was these values that prompted him to treat his yaks with gentleness. He would encourage the yaks by making special sounds to them. He had devised his own way of showing them appreciation or scolding them off certain trails. 'Rr-r-r-r!' he would go, or 'Chhe-che-che-che!'

The yaks were moody creatures. Long-haired and woolly, with horns that curved outwards and up, they were smaller in size than their wild cousins whom Tenzing saw grazing on the upper hill slopes, among the snow and boulders. Some days, they did not give him any cause for alarm, and he came home to eat and sleep peacefully soon after dusk. But on other days, they would give him anxious moments, as they lingered among the areas with the tastiest stretches of green, or strayed off towards the wild herds. He would then have to scramble quickly up and down the steep paths, calling the yaks by name, and promising them fine treats if they returned. Yaks are highly valued by the Tibetans for their milk and butter, *chhurpi* cheese, warm wool and fur.

Tenzing and his yaks inhabited an area that is often referred to as the 'roof of the world' because it is much higher than any other region on the globe. During his customary walk with the yaks he would pass hundreds of fluttering prayer flags in yellow, white, red, green and blue, strung together and hung alongside the mountain paths. When their path led up to a monastery or holy shrine, Tenzing would also see *mani* stones, or rocks and boulders that had been carved with the syllables of the Tibetan Buddhist mantra '*Om Mani Padme Hum*'. These stones were placed by wanderers, travellers and pilgrims and over time, they had become a long continuous stretch leading to each holy place.

The eleventh child in a family of thirteen children, Tenzing was the son of Ghang La Mingma, a yak herder from the Sherpa community, and his wife Dokmo Kinzom. He was born in 1914 in a village called Tsa-chu, near Makalu in East Nepal. Unfortunately, the cold and inhospitable weather conditions in which the family had to survive, in remote villages with little access to health care, led to his losing many of his siblings while they were still very young. Although Tenzing's exact date of birth was never recorded, as an adult he surmised—with the help of what his mother recalled of the weather and the crop cycle—that it must have been late May. His feat of completing the ascent to the peak of Everest on May 29, 1953, led him to declare that as his birthday from then onwards!

Tenzing's family had a deep respect for the lamas and monks who are the anchors of Tibetan Buddhism. He had been named Namgyal Wangdi after his birth. Some years later, when his parents took him on a pilgrimage to the famous Rongbuk Monastery, they had a special audience with its head lama and founder. This monastery is the highest place of worship in the world, at an altitude of 5100 m above sea level, and all climbers to Everest who take this route pause at this monastery to receive blessings for their trek. The head lama at Rongbuk foresaw a great future for the child, and advised his parents to change his name to Ngawang Tenzin Norbu. These were high blessings to receive from the highly revered lama—Tenzing Norgay's name means a wealthy and fortunate follower of religion.

Living at the highest altitudes on earth, where the air is much more difficult to breathe on account of lower levels of oxygen in the rarefied atmosphere, Sherpas are specially equipped to climb up and down the mountains. Tenzing and his family belonged to an ethnic group indigenous to Tibet and found primarily on the southern slopes of the Himalayas, including Nepal.

Sherpas worship a pantheon of deities in addition to being primarily Buddhists. The gods and goddesses are invoked to deal with everyday problems. For instance, one religious story of the Sherpas ascribes five daughters to father Lohla Tebu and mother Menthang. These are Tashi Tseringma who gives longevity, Miyo Longsma who gives food, Tekar Longsama who gives good fortune, Chopen Dinsangma who gives wealth and Thingi Shelsangma who gives telepathic powers.

Equipped with physical strength well-suited and acclimatised to high altitude climbing, and protected by the beliefs that have been shaped by their forefathers, Sherpas have an amazing record of climbing in the Himalayas. The records for the fastest Everest ascent as well as the most number of climbs made by one person, are both held by Sherpas.

As a child, when Tenzing gazed dreamily at the peak which towered higher than all the others, he did not really wish to conquer it—this was not the way he had been brought up. What he felt was much closer to a deep respect, almost a prayer. But within his dreams, the seeds of curiosity about life beyond the valley where he lived, most definitely existed. As a boy, he ran away from home twice to the big city of Kathmandu. But being on his own in a new place where he had to work very hard to scrape together a meal for himself, was a scary and lonely existence, and he returned once again to his yak herd.

By the time Tenzing was in his teens, the Western

curiosity, or in fact, obsession, with Everest was bringing many climbing teams to Kathmandu. All of them depended on Sherpas to be their highly skilled porters, cooks, base camp managers and mountain guides. For the first time, it seemed as if fate was giving Tenzing a chance to bridge the gap between the remote mountainous region where he grew up and the much larger world beyond. In 1935, at the age of twenty-one, Tenzing was chosen for his first expedition, although he couldn't yet speak a word of English and told his hirers by means of gestures that he had no certificate from the Himalayan Club.

Twenty years later, this formerly illiterate yak herder had not only scaled the world's tallest mountain, but also earned the respect of world leaders and common people everywhere with his wide and cheerful smile, and his complete absence of fear. He described the first moment after his conquest thus: 'It was such a sight as I had never seen before, and would never see again— wild, wonderful, and terrible. But terror was not what I felt. I loved the mountains too well for that. I loved Everest too well.'

M.F. Husain

(b. 1915)

Maqbool Fida Husain, or M.F. Husain as he is best known, is a world-famous painter and one of India's most successful artists. Born in Pandharpur, Husain spent his childhood in Indore. He arrived in Mumbai in 1935, where he studied at the J.J. School of Art. He began his career by painting hoardings for Hindi films. In 1948, he was invited by F.N. Souza to form the Progressive Artists' Group. He eventually became a leading figure in shaping contemporary Indian art. In 1955, he was awarded the Padma Shri. Husain was invited to the Sao Paulo Biennial exhibition of art along with Pablo Picasso in 1971. He has also received the Padma Bhushan in 1973 and the Padma Vibhushan in 1989, besides being nominated to the Rajya Sabha in 1986. Since 1996, his work became the subject of controversy when he was attacked by some Hindu fundamentalist groups for nude depiction of gods and goddesses. The controversy and subsequent litigation has led to Husain living the life of an exile in Dubai and London in recent times. Apart from his work on canvas, Husain has also made films like *Through the Eyes of a Painter* that won the Golden Bear Award at the Berlin Film Festival, *Gajagamini* and *Meenaxi: A Tale of Three Cities*.

The boy was playing in the street with a group of friends, when he was called. 'Maqbool! Come quickly! Dada wants you.'

Turning from the street where he had been running and hiding inside the narrow crevices between houses, the boy went into the house where all his relatives were gathered in an anxious state. 'He would not even sip a drop of the pomegranate juice!' an aunt was saying to another in a hushed voice. Another wept softly at regular intervals as she read aloud a chapter of *Yaasin* from the scriptures.

His uncles were grouped around his grandfather's bed.

When Maqbool reached his grandfather's room, slightly out of breath from running, and sweating from his recent exertion, the uncles made way, patting him on the shoulders and making him sit next to the bed on which the old man lay. 'Here's Maqbool,' they told the old gentleman. Then they left the two alone.

Sitting alone at his beloved grandfather's bedside, the boy watched with unblinking eyes as a tear trickled from his Dada's firmly closed eyes. The tear stopped at the edge of the old man's beard. The room was full of objects that yearned for his Dada's presence. The black fur topi that his grandfather always wore was pegged to the wall. The brown *achkan* or long coat that was his Dada's usual garment swayed slightly in the breeze coming through the half open window. As the boy looked at the *achkan* he felt it was pleading that Dada should

110

wear it one more time and walk away to a far-off land.

However, even as the *achkan* moved, Dada's hand, which had always emerged from the sleeve of the *achkan* turned still. The boy remembered walking the streets, holding his grandfather's finger with his own thin hand. He sat still, slowly realising that his grandfather would no longer lead him by the finger through the streets of the town.

Maqbool Fida Husain was born on September 17, 1915 in Pandharpur, Maharashtra. Pandharpur is a pilgrim town, dotted with many temples, the most famous of these being the Vitthal and Rukmabai temple in the centre of the town.

Husain's life was hit by tragedy at a very young age as his mother passed away when he was just one-and-a-half years old. His mother had been the one to give him his name Maqbool. After her death, the infant Husain was in the care of several members of the extended family, till his father remarried and the family moved to Indore.

The Malwa region of Madhya Pradesh, in which the town of Indore is situated, was the backdrop for the formative years of Husain's childhood, providing him with the most intimate glimpses of people at work and play, as well as a countryside of lush green fields, dotted with villages. The town itself had many historic buildings and bustling market places. Husain's family lived in a house whose window afforded him a clear view of people on the street below and across the street in the house opposite his own.

Husain's early memories of this setting show the observant and impressionable nature of his childhood. As he has said in the semi-autobiographical book, *M.F. Husain Where Art Thou*, he would stand for hours at the window 'reading the stories on the faces of the people passing through the street.' He watched how a blind woman who lived with her two grown-up sons in the house across the street picked up ordinary household objects with a 'prescient precision'. The sound of vessels being washed with a scraping sound, or a *lota* being filled and emptied of water became familiar symbols of the people around him. His artist's eye and mind was recording everything.

The Dada whose finger he clutched to make his way through the streets of the town was one of the first family members who encouraged him to draw. Husain took up pencil and paper, paint and brush quite early in life, but his first visual expression was not just painting. It was the calligraphy of the Persian-Arabic-Urdu script that he learned while staying at an uncle's house in Baroda.

By the time he was a teenager, he had begun to go further afield in search of subjects to draw. The tall and lanky boy would strap up his drawing and painting gear to a bicycle and go out of town into the rural setting of the countryside. His fascination with horses began at this time, as he watched them in both, the ceremonial setting of the British Raj and the Holkar kingdom, as well as the rustic setting of the villages around Indore.

Later, this would be expressed in his series of paintings of horses in motion.

Although Husain's emergence as an artist was only completed after he had gone to Mumbai at the age of twenty and studied at the J.J. School of Art, the period of his childhood is a rich reservoir of memories and impressions that fed his creative instinct. While he was growing up, his schooling was erratic, but he was fully exposed to the theatre of life. His life has been through many distinct periods, including the freedom struggle, and the upheavals that have characterised independent India. There are also the controversies generated by his paintings from the time he was eighty-one years old. Through it all, he has been distinctly aware of the warp and weft with which life is woven in India—the pilgrims that make their way to shrines, the tales and epics that nourish the popular imagination, the strength and aspirations of ordinary people.

As M.F. Husain says himself, while he has become a global brand name for art, a public figure who is as much reviled as respected, and an international icon, he still remembers what it felt like to be a little boy learning to walk on the streets holding his grandfather's finger.

Satyajit Ray

(1921 – 1993)

Satyajit Ray is not only one of India's best-known film-makers, he is also counted among the great masters of world cinema. A multi-talented man who was a wonderful illustrator and writer, he also created the musical score for his own films. Satyajit Ray belonged to a family strongly associated with the world of arts and letters. His films are known for their deep humanism and the minute details of life as it is lived at many levels in India. Ray's education at the Vishwa-Bharati University at Shantiniketan, founded by Rabindranath Tagore, brought him into direct contact with some of the finest artists of the Indian tradition such as Nandalal Bose and Benode Behari Mukherjee. He worked as a commercial artist in his youth and an encounter with the French film-maker Jean Renoir was important in drawing him to the art of film-making, as was the Italian neo-realist film *Bicycle Thieves* directed by Vittorio de Sica that he saw many times while he was on a visit to London. He directed thirty-seven films that include feature films, documentaries and shorts. The Apu trilogy consisting of *Pather Panchali*, *Aparajito* and *Apur Sansar* are his best-known films even fifty years after they were made, while others, like *Goopy Gyne, Bagha Byne,* have created unforgettable magic for generations of children.

As the boy came running in from the street, he could hear the sound of his mother's sewing machine. 'Ma!' he called. 'Bibhu has a new whistle—the kind that can blow up to five different notes.'

'Really?' asked his mother, straightening her back and smiling at him from the chair where she sat bent in concentration over her stitching for many hours of the day. 'Did he let you try it?'

'Yes!' said the boy. 'And do you know, even though the whistle belongs to him, it was I who discovered all the five notes!'

'That's wonderful, son,' said the mother. She began preparing another piece of cloth to slide under the sewing machine needle.

The boy brought his face close to his mother's, and looked deep into her eyes. 'Don't start sewing again, please, Ma?' he asked entreatingly. 'You look so tired,' he continued, as if in explanation.

His mother laughed, and shook her head, and began putting away the cloth she had just brought out. 'You are a clever fellow!' she said. "You really know how to convince me. Do you want to listen to a story, then?"

'Oh yes!' said her son Satyajit. 'Tell me one of Baba's. I want a really funny one.'

Smiling at his request, his mother removed a well-thumbed book from a nearby shelf. Then, sitting down with him leaning into her lap, she began to read ...

Satyajit Ray was born on May 2, 1921 into a home where books and papers were the most natural things in the world—next only to food and water. His grandfather, Upendra Kishore Ray, who died six years before Satyajit was born, had been a well-known writer, painter and composer. Upendra Kishore's press, U. Ray & Sons did pioneering work in printing, perfecting the techniques of half-tone block making, so vital in getting pictures to look realistic on paper. Satyajit's grandfather was also an accomplished violin player.

Upendra Kishore's eldest son Sukumar Ray was Satyajit Ray's father. He was sent to study printing technology in England in order to enable him to join the family business. He wrote and illustrated nonsense literature and verse in Bengali, like Lewis Carroll and Edward Lear had done in English. His poems, stories and illustrations appeared regularly in *Sandesh*, a children's magazine published and printed by Upendra Kishore Ray.

Tragically, Sukumar Ray was struck by the much-dreaded *kala-azar* disease the very year of Satyajit's birth, and he passed away when his son was barely three. However, Satyajit Ray's earliest memories included the smells, sounds and sights associated with the block-making and printing process, and a profusion of books and journals.

The Ray family was part of the Bengal Renaissance—the vast movement for social reform that marked Bengali society in the late nineteenth and early twentieth centuries. Questioning existing orthodoxy with respect to women, marriage, the dowry system, the caste system and religion, the Bengal Renaissance was expressed in an intellectual flowering similar to that of Europe in the sixteenth century. It marked the transition of Bengali society from the rigidly traditional to the modern, and was led by the Brahmo Samaj, an organisation that the Ray family had joined in the 1880s. This sect founded by noted reformer Raja Ram Mohan Roy challenged Christian Puritanism, and Western literature as well as orthodox Hindu practices, such as *sati*. Growing up under the influence of such a powerful social awakening, Satyajit Ray was bound to develop a cosmopolitan and rational outlook, and these remained his core values throughout his life.

After his father's death, his mother Suprabha Ray found it difficult to make ends meet on the meagre income she earned as a seamstress, and by teaching needlework. Around three years after his father had passed away, the family printing business was sold, and Satyajit and his mother left the large and comfortable house they had lived in for Suprabha's brother's house, where Satyajit was exposed to the much larger circle of extended family and relatives. It was here that he met a distant cousin Bijoya some years later. Bijoya was the youngest daughter of Charuchandra Das, Satyajit's eldest maternal uncle. When Satyajit was ten years old, Bijoya's father died and she came to live in the house of his step-brother, where Satyajit and his mother were already staying.

The cousins became close to each other, owing also

to a shared interest in Western classical music and films. Bijoya was the elder by four years. Whatever it was that Satyajit tried his hand at, whether it was collecting gramophone records, or writing short stories and novelettes for children, or drawing and sketching, Bijoya always encouraged him. Much later, when Satyajit was twenty-seven years old, he and Bijoya were married and their creative partnership became a lifelong one, with her contributing in unimaginable ways towards his films, from being the first one to hear his scripts, to finding the child actor who played Apu in *Pather Panchali*, to costume design and many other things.

Satyajit began going to school only at the age of eight. Till then, his mother had been his only teacher. He started attending Ballygunj government school, but did not overly distinguish himself in studies. On the other hand, his exposure to the outside world due to his extended family with varied interests was continuing. Satyajit not only spent time with his maternal uncles, his paternal uncles and aunts, too, had a hand in his growing up. One day, an uncle and aunt had taken him to see the Kolkata (formerly Calcutta) port, which was very exciting because of the vessels of different colours and sizes anchored at the shipyard. On the way back from what was quite a tiring trip, they stopped to eat at a restaurant, and the meal concluded with ice-cream. Eager to eat it, Satyajit found that it was too cold for consumption. To his uncle and aunt's surprise, Satyajit suddenly left his seat and ran up to the waiter who had just served them. The bemused aunt and uncle watched the man bend down while Satyajit spoke to him in whispers, then begin laughing aloud. When questioned about what had caused him to laugh, the waiter came up to the table and said, 'He wants me to take the ice-cream back and heat it up!'

As a schoolboy, Satyajit became addicted to films. He devoured any information about films in magazines and newspapers, and he and Bijoya were particularly fond of Hollywood musicals. He read *Picturegoer* and *Photoplay*, two magazines that were the favourites of film buffs. By the time he finished school at the age of fifteen, his interest in films was extremely well-marked, as was his passion for Western classical music.

On his mother's insistence, Satyajit joined Presidency College as a teenager, to study science. But his classes hardly held his interest. He was more interested in the world of movies. As he has described, 'It was the most exciting period. I had discovered a new world. When I watched a film I was not only interested in what the stars were doing, but also in observing how the camera was being deployed, when the cuts came, how the narrative unfolded, and what were the characteristics that distinguished the work of one director from another.'

Years later, he unveiled how the craft of film-making had actually shaped his life, 'Apart from the actual creative work, film-making is exciting because it brings me closer to my country and my people. Each film contributes to a process of self-education, making me conscious of the enormous diversity of life around me. I find myself trying, through my films, to trace the underlying pattern that binds this life together ... Before I made my first film, *Pather Panchali*, I had only a superficial knowledge of what life in a Bengali village was like. Now I know a good deal about it. I know its soil, its seasons, its trees and forests and flowers, I know how the man in the field works and how the women at the well gossip, and I know the children out in the sun and the rain, behaving as all children in all parts of the world do.'

Che Guevara

(1928 – 1967)

Che Guevara is the name by which Ernesto Guevara de la Serna is widely known throughout the world. He was also referred to as El Che or just Che by his many followers. Born in Argentina, Che was a Marxist revolutionary and leader of the Cuban revolution who died trying to bring about his ideal of liberating Latin America from US control and influence.

Che's ideas for revolution were shaped by his experiences as a young man, when as a student of medicine, he travelled with a friend throughout South America. This brought him close to the people and he was much struck by the socio-economic inequalities that led to millions living in miserable conditions. Convinced that this inequality could only be remedied by revolution, Che studied Marxism in depth and travelled to Guatemala to learn about the reforms being implemented there by President Jacobo Arbenz Guzmán. He met Fidel Castro in 1956, and became a part of the force that led to the defeat of General Batista in Cuba in 1959, and the establishment of a communist government. For a few years, he represented Cuba on the international stage, before deciding to leave Cuba for Bolivia in 1965 to usher in a revolution in that country with the help of guerilla forces. Here, in the town of La Higuera near Vallegrande, Che

Guevara was executed in a military operation supported by the CIA and the US army special forces. The legend of Che grew greater after his death, with him becoming an icon of socialist revolutionary movements and a much-loved image in modern pop culture.

The work at the vineyard was meant to have been a mere vacation job for the two boys from a well-off family. When he took on Ernesto and Roberto, the vineyard owner assumed that they would work along with the other peasants during the harvesting, and be glad to have earned some extra money for themselves and their friends. Instead, as he looked into the face of the teenager fighting for the wages of the vineyard labourers, he saw something completely different from youthful arrogance—he saw the anger of a man who would do anything to save his fellow workers from being underpaid and exploited.

'You cannot pay the workers less than what you

had promised at the start of the harvest,' repeated the boy to the vineyard owner.

The vineyard owner felt cornered before the watchful eyes of a dozen or more farm hands. How should he handle this youngster? In desperation, he tried a different tack. 'Why speak for all the rest of them?' he taunted. 'Speak for yourself. How can I pay you for all the days when you missed so many days on account of illness?'

The crafty vineyard owner had scored a significant goal. Under this attack, the boy seemed to retreat slightly—after all, it was true that his asthma attacks had kept him from coming on all the days of his summer job. 'You do not have to pay me full wages,' he said. 'Just pay each one of them what you promised and what they have earned.'

The fourteen-year-old who argued for men and women much older than himself was born on June 14, 1928, the son of Ernesto Guevara Lynch and Celia de la Serna y Llosa, in Rosario, Argentina. In those days, Argentina had not been hit by the Great Depression and was quite a prosperous country, where Ernesto's grandparents had belonged to the wealthy aristocracy. His father's ancestors had lived in Argentina for twelve generations, making them nobles in a land filling up with recently-arrived immigrants. His mother's family owned such extensive property that her share of the fortune was enough for Ernesto's family to live on for many years, in spite of his father trying out several failed businesses in the years he was growing up.

Ernesto spent the first weeks of his life in Rosario, a place where he was born by sheer chance. Leaving the area of Misiones, where they lived, to go to Buenos Aires, his parents decided to stop in Rosario as his mother was not feeling well. Here, his mother gave birth to him in a house on 480 Entre Rios St. Some weeks later, after she was fit to travel, the couple went back home to Misiones with their first-born. Here his father had a mate plantation in Port Caraguatay, close to the border of Brazil and Paraguay. Ernesto learnt to take his first steps in a wooden house perched on a hill.

Just a few weeks before his second birthday, on May 2, 1930, Ernesto suffered his first attack of asthma—a frightening event that considerably influenced relationships within his family. His father held his mother responsible for the attack, on the grounds of his mother having taken him swimming on a cold and rainy day. Although this was possibly not the only cause, since asthma has subsequently been found to have very strong hereditary causes, his mother was consumed by guilt and anguish at seeing her child suffer. She remembered having asthma attacks herself as a child, and felt doubly responsible for her child's pain. This made her extremely protective and loving towards her son, a feeling that did not lessen in any way after the birth of her other children, son Roberto, daughters Ana Maria and Celia, and much later, a son named Juan Martin.

In order to live in a warm and dry climate suited to Ernesto's asthmatic condition, the family moved to Alta Gracia, a summer resort town 40 kilometres from the city of Cordoba, situated at the foot of the Sierra Chica mountains and with an elevation of almost 600 metres above sea level. This is where Ernesto grew up, his family and home relatively secure and untroubled in the midst of the political and economic instability of Argentina.

Both his parents influenced Ernesto in different ways. His mother Celia, who had been raised by her older sister and brother-in-law, both card-carrying members of the Argentine communist party, was strongly liberal in her views. Although she had grown up with a conservative Catholic education, her subsequent time as a young woman in her sister's home had made her a freethinking radical, with socialist and feminist views that made her unusual in that time. Meetings at her home were common during the many struggles of Argentine women in the 1920s and 1930s. Because of his illness, Celia taught Ernesto at home, instilling in him a lifelong love of books and learning. He not only learned to read and write on her lap, but also learned French and poetry.

His father was a slightly aloof and distant figure who did not concern himself much with home and family, preferring instead to spend long hours at the Sierras Hotel, a kind of club for the wealthy. He had a different influence on Ernesto. He conveyed to his son a great love of sports and exercise, and convinced the boy that he could overcome the limitations and hardships imposed by his illness through will power alone. Enjoying the outdoors and games as much as both his athletic parents did, little Ernesto developed uncommon will power to be able to sustain his physical activity in spite of the asthma attacks it triggered. He learnt to swim and ride, and became very good at rugby, a game that taught him teamwork, leadership and observation, apart from strengthening his willpower.

The open house that his family maintained also made Ernesto completely disregard social and economic differences. He could make friends with anyone—a caddy from the Alta Gracia golf club, a serving boy from a hotel, the children of construction workers from the sites of his father's real-estate company, and slum children near the family's rented villas. Ernesto's friends came in all shapes, sizes and colours: some white and middle-class like him, others poor and dark-skinned. To him, they were truly all one. It was no wonder that this chess-playing child, who had read Freud and Marx, Alexandre Dumas, Robert Louis Stevenson, Jack London, Jules Verne, Cervantes and Anatole France, Pablo Neruda and the Spanish poets, Machado and Garcia Lorca, before he turned eighteen should feel impelled to use his knowledge for the good of humanity as a whole.

If there is one quote that captures the character of the grown Ernesto Guevara, whom the world knew simply as Che, it is the letter he wrote to his children before leaving on the journey that finally killed him. 'Above all, always remain capable of feeling deeply whatever injustice is committed against anyone in any part of the world. This is the finest quality of a revolutionary.'

Neil Armstrong

(b. 1930)

Neil Armstrong is not only the first man to have walked on the surface of the moon, he is also one of only twelve people who have walked on the moon's surface in the twentieth century. A lunar crater close to the Apollo 11 landing site is named after him. This former American astronaut, test pilot, university professor and naval aviator was the command pilot for the Gemini 8 space flight in 1966, and successfully docked two spacecraft together with pilot David Scott. During the Apollo 11 mission, Armstrong and Buzz Aldrin spent two-and-a-half hours exploring the lunar surface on July 20, 1969. Armstrong served in the US Navy before becoming an astronaut and was a pilot in the Korean War. He was also a test pilot at the Dryden Flight Research Center, where he flew over 900 flights in a variety of aircraft. A graduate of Purdue University, Armstrong has received many honours including the Presidential Medal of Freedom; the Congressional Space Medal of Honor; the Explorers Club Medal; the Robert H. Goddard Memorial Trophy; the NASA Distinguished Service Medal; the Harmon International Aviation Trophy; the Royal Geographic Society's Gold Medal; the Federation Aeronautique Internationale's Gold Space Medal; and the American Astronautical Society Flight Achievement Award.

'I've finished sweeping the back of the store, Mr Brading!' called the youngest employee of Rhine and Brading's pharmacy.

'What about those cartons that arrived last evening? Are you done with them as well?' asked his boss Dick Brading from behind the counter at the front of the shop.

'I did those first thing I got in,' said the boy cheerfully, coming out to the front, tucking his shirt more firmly into the waistband of his jeans. 'May I have my money now?'

'Sure thing, son,' said Mr Brading, with a grin. 'I can see by the look of you that it's one of them afternoons! Off down the old brewery road, aren't you?'

'Yes, sir!' said the small and slightly built teenager, smiling brightly back at his boss. 'I'm going to fly!' He accepted the coins that Mr Brading was handing out to him, and pocketed them. Then he got on to his bicycle and began cycling at a furious pace down the old brewery road to the Wapak Flying Service. Here, Charles Finkenbine waited to receive his nine dollars for an hour of flying—all in change! People in Wapakoneta, Ohio, in 1944, were aware of this teenager's passion for flying. A passion that made him work for 40 cents an hour so he could save it up and spend it on flying lessons on Finkenbine's light planes a few afternoons a month.

When Neil Armstrong got his pilot's license on August 5, 1946, it was his sixteenth birthday and he didn't yet have an automobile driver's license!

Neil Armstrong was born on August 5, 1930, on his grandparents' farm in Auglaize County, Ohio, the son of Stephen Koenig Armstrong and Viola Engel Armstrong. His father worked for the Ohio government and the family moved around the state quite a bit before settling down in Wapakoneta, where Neil spent most of his childhood. Neil was the eldest of three children, and the early years of his life coincided with the Depression in the US—a period of deep economic crisis—when millions of people lost their jobs and homes, and families found it hard to put food on the table. In this period of hardship, free-spending Americans had to learn the values of saving and frugal living.

If there was a set of values that governed Neil Armstrong's childhood, it was hard work, being cheerful, saving money, counting one's blessings because things could be a lot worse, praying for things to be better, getting educated to improve one's circumstances and avoiding the greatest sin known to man—laziness! By these parameters, Neil and his siblings had to help at home with chores and errands, earn money at odd jobs and be careful to ask for only the things that the family could afford.

Even as a very small child, Neil had a recurring dream in which he hovered over the ground, as if in flight. Nothing much happened though! He neither had the sensation of soaring through the air, or of falling, just hovering, as if suspended above the ground. When he tried to do it in waking moments, he failed, of course! But his love and near-obsession with all types of aircraft began when he was six years old and took his first flight, in a Ford Tri-Motor Tin Goose.

His fascination with planes led Neil to build a small wind tunnel in the basement of his home where he performed experiments on model planes and simulated their short flights. His family and everyone who knew him soon began thinking of him as an expert on aircrafts and aviation, even though he was still a boy. Although he was more interested in airplanes than in people, Neil made an active and energetic Boy Scout, earning points and moving up the ladder to finally become an Eagle. When he uttered his famous words after the moon landing to the Mission Control at Houston, 'Houston, Tranquility Base here. The Eagle has landed!', the primary reference was to the lunar module which was called the *Eagle*, but somewhere he must have also remembered his status as an Eagle Scout.

Neil Armstrong attended Blume High School in Wapakoneta with his sister June and brother Dean. One of his childhood jobs was at a bakery. He got this job because he was small enough to be put bodily into the bread dough-mixing vats to clean them at night! Such hard work may be unimaginable for middle-class children in today's US, but for Neil and his brother and sister, it was one more way of helping out the family in the days of the Depression.

His mother, a soft-spoken woman with interests in

music and literature, was used to the extraordinary passion with which he approached the subject of aircrafts and flying. But the harsh period of the Depression had made her wonder whether such a passion was enough to take Neil to college. In fact, both parents thought that extraordinary blessings would need to rain on them before their kids could go to college.

One day, when an excited young Neil ran home to tell his mother that he had won a Navy scholarship to go to Purdue University, she was so astonished and overcome that she dropped a big jar of raspberry jam on her right foot and broke her big toe!

When Neil got his pilot's license, he was small and slight and looked around TWELVE years old. Headed for Purdue University, he was a fresh-faced boy of seventeen.

Armstrong studied Aeronautical Engineering at Purdue. He would later go on to distinguish himself as a pilot flying warplanes in combat, as a test pilot, and as an astronaut who successfully led two path-breaking missions for American space exploration. His famous quote on first taking a step on the moon, 'That's one small step for [a] man, one giant leap for mankind' has become an enduring description of that historic moment.

And to think it all started with a dream in which he 'hovered' like a rocket suspended in space!

John Lennon

(1940 – 1980)

The Beatles are widely regarded as one of the most successful rock groups of all time. From their emergence in 1960-61 to the present day, their records and songs continue to draw a worldwide following. John Lennon founded the band along with Paul McCartney, his friend from the days they were both growing up in Liverpool. John Lennon was awarded an Academy Award, Grammy Award, an MBE from the British government, and was widely acclaimed for his songs, music, pen-and-ink cartoons, writings and political activism. John Lennon is especially remembered for his visionary lyrics in songs he wrote after the Beatles split up, such as 'Imagine' and his anti-war efforts through songs like 'Give Peace A Chance'. Lennon was married twice, first to Cynthia Powell, with whom he had a son called Julian, and then to avant-garde artist Yoko Ono, mother of his son Sean. Lennon was tragically murdered by a mentally unstable fan called Mark David Chapman, in New York City on December 8, 1980.

———————————

The boy was completely absorbed in the tunes he was able to pluck out of his guitar. His aunt called him to the dinner table but he seemed reluctant to keep his new instrument aside even for the time it would take to bolt his food and rush back to continue his experiments. Her practical and earnest nature was considerably irritated by such wanton disobedience of the rules of the house. Aunt Mimi walked up and snatched the guitar from John's fingers. 'You can play once you've eaten dinner!' she said fiercely as he looked up at her in surprise and alarm.

As his experimentation on the chords and strings of the guitar increased, the noise levels in the house called Mendips on Menlove Avenue in Liverpool, where John Lennon lived with his aunt Mimi and uncle George Smith, also went up considerably. Unable to bear this constant twanging, Mimi banished her nephew outside to the front porch, telling him, 'The guitar's all very well, John, but you'll never make a living out of it.'

The reason why John Lennon came to be staying with his aunt and uncle instead of his parents was the failed family relationships that made his childhood such a difficult one. He was born in the middle of an air raid in World War II in Liverpool on the night of October 9, 1940. His mother Julia was at her father's home and his father Alfred was at sea at the time of his birth. Julia had married Alfred against the wishes of her parents and four sisters. He was a merchant seaman who was on shore leave at rare intervals, and had gone to sea the day after their wedding.

Julia gave her son John the middle name Winston in tribute to Prime Minister Churchill. Since Julia had no income, she continued to stay with her father, and in the long absences of her husband, she met and fell in love with John 'Bobby' Dykins, with whom she moved into a small flat. Julia's sister Mimi strongly disapproved of such an arrangement. In those much more conservative times in England, she considered this to be 'living in sin' and a bad influence on the small John. Determined to wrest control of her nephew, Aunt Mimi made a representation to the Liverpool social services that resulted in her getting charge of John.

By 1946 John lived with George and Mimi Smith. His father Alfred came to visit him on one of his periods of shore leave. He took the boy from Aunt Mimi's house, ostensibly for a trip to Blackpool, but secretly intending to take him to New Zealand where they would begin a new life together. John's mother and Bobby Dykins followed the duo and challenged Alfred. His father asked the five-year-old John to make a particularly difficult decision: to choose between him and his mother. John twice chose his father, but when his mother started walking away, he began to cry and followed her instead. How much such painful choices must have ravaged the feelings of an unusually sensitive child can only be estimated by John's later songs.

Back in Liverpool, John grew up in the peculiar situation of having 'home' mean his aunt's house, from where he was allowed occasional visits to see his mother, and his two half-sisters, born after his mother set up home with Bobby Dykins. Julia's other sisters sympathised with John's predicament and encouraged and facilitated his visits to his own mother. He was also surrounded by cousins and extended family. However, his childhood was dominated by two contrasting environments—the orderly, predictable, comfortable but boring home of Aunt Mimi, and the warm and free-wheeling home of Julia and Bobby. His Aunt Mimi called his mother's house 'The House of Sin' and her own home 'The House of Correction.'

John's talent emerged early, as he showed great promise in writing and telling stories, drawing, and music. But he was so naughty that he was expelled from kindergarten! He graduated from Quarry Bank High School without distinguishing himself in any way, even though he was a bright and intelligent boy. It was the efforts of Aunt Mimi and the headmaster, along with a portfolio of his work, that got him accepted at Art College.

During his schooldays, after he turned eleven and was able to make his own way to school, he began dropping in to see his mother on the way home, thus getting to know her better. So began a very happy period for him when he could break rules, or just have fun, without the fear of being scolded, or upsetting anyone. In these years, John was a happy-go-lucky boy who climbed trees, earned pocket money collecting golf balls at a local golf course, and playing cricket in the street.

By the time he was a teenager, Aunt Mimi had reluctantly accepted that he wanted to spend more time with his own family, and she allowed him to go on holiday with his mother and sisters. John knew by this time that he was happiest with his real mother. It felt strange to feel guilty about betraying Aunt Mimi and her strong opinions of his mother's character, but he could not help the way he felt.

His mother was the single most influential figure in shaping his talent and his immense curiosity about the world. From her he learnt to draw pen-and-ink cartoons, paint pictures and create storybooks bound with red knitting wool. She would take him on trips to the city with his sisters where they travelled on the train which went under the Mersey river. She could play the ukulele, the accordion and the mother-of-pearl banjo she had inherited from her father. John listened to and grew to love a wide repertoire of songs and music. Julia dressed up in dramatic clothes, performed for her children's entertainment, impersonated a famous comedian, and named her cat after Elvis Presley. As a musician and entertainer, John couldn't have asked for a more inspiring parent.

Then came the tragedy that changed John's life forever, and marked his passage from teenage to adulthood in a single moment. His mother, who had taken his young friend Paul McCartney under her wing when Paul had lost his mother, was killed in a tragic accident in July 1958. She had been to visit her sister Mimi and was on her way to the bus stop to return home when a car driven by a drunken off-duty police officer ran her over. Seventeen-year-old John heard of his mother's death from a policeman.

Aunt Mimi recalled the awful moments that followed the tragedy, that John 'just went to his room into a shell.' John was shattered to lose her at a time when he had just begun to reestablish a relationship with her, after the trauma of their earlier separation by circumstances. The intense pain he felt poured itself out in later songs, including one he wrote specially for her, called 'Julia'.

As for Aunt Mimi's warning about the guitar— many years later, after the Beatles were world-famous, John Lennon presented his aunt with a silver platter engraved with the words, 'The guitar's all very well, John, but you'll never make a living out of it.'

Pelé

(b. 1940)

Edson Arantes do Nascimento, or Pelé as he is known the world over, is perhaps the best footballer the world has known. His skill, great courage and appetite for the game, and understanding of its nuances made him invaluable to Brazil's national team. As a teenager, he contributed to Brazil's World Cup victory in 1958. Pelé was athletic enough to play any sport, or perform anywhere on the field, but he is indelibly imprinted on public memory as the inside-left forward wearing a number 10 shirt. Pelé's game skills included great footwork, effortless balance around defenders, and an unerring ability with headers. It was no wonder that he scored seventy-seven goals for Brazil in the ninety-two matches he played for his country. He is the only player to have been thrice in a FIFA World Cup-winning side. Pelé played in the North American Soccer League from 1975-77. He retired from soccer after having scored more than 1200 goals—an astounding number. After retiring from soccer, Pelé has been active as a businessman and campaigner for several causes. In 1978, he was awarded the International Peace Award, and in 1980, he was named athlete of the century. In 1993, Pelé was inducted into the National Soccer Hall of Fame. He has also been an ambassador of sports in Brazil. He has worked extensively for children's causes through the UNICEF.

It was absolutely useless. Not one of the boys who were elder and bigger than Edson Arantes do Nascimento could do anything to best him in the football games they played on the school ground, in the streets, or in any square yard of open ground. The small and wiry boy spun circles around them, seeming to charm the football away from their leaden feet. Frustrated at trying to explain this phenomenon, one of them thought he had found a way to check the boy's onslaught.

'Pelé!' he called. Then, again, 'Pelé, Pelé, Pelé!'

When the other boys around him began laughing, Edson looked around. 'Are you calling me?' he asked. 'Why don't you call me by my name? What does Pelé mean?'

'Nothing!' said his tormentor. 'It means nothing. Why, do you think you should have a grand title?'

'Don't call me that again,' said the small footballer, who had just a few minutes ago been running like a bolt of lightning around the field. His chest was heaving with anger and exertion. 'What if I do?' asked the older boy, emboldened by his friends standing all around them. 'I'll fight you!' declared Edson, rushing forward and butting his teasing friend in the stomach.

That childhood fight was soon resolved, but the name Pelé was to achieve immortality as it began to ring across the football stadiums of the world. When the greatest football player of the world scored a goal, or made an exceptional recovery of the ball from his opponents, the crowd cheered him by the name with which he was best known—a childhood tag given by a teasing friend.

Pelé was born on October 23, 1940, to Dondinho and Celeste Nascimento in Tres Coracos, a poor small town in the state of Minas Gerais in Southeastern Brazil. Growing up in a very poor family, he was deprived of many material necessities, but never lacked affection. His parents fondly called him Dico. His father was always a role model for Pelé. Pelé learnt the game of football from him. His father was a local professional soccer player very much admired for his feat of having scored five goals with his head in one game!

However, Dondinho's career as a decent centre-forward came to a sudden end due to a fractured leg. The family's struggle for survival became more intense. Pelé's schooling was erratic. As a very young boy, he spent equal time playing football on the streets with his friends, and shining shoes to earn money for his family. He would be happy if his mother had cooked extra food in the evening when he came home for dinner after hours spent on the streets. He would wash with tap water any injury he had sustained on the field and run right back into the game, or sometimes just rub impatiently at the bruise, and keep going. All the tender care that children today take for granted from their parents and families could not be part of Pelé's young life. Life was tough, but it was also happy, filled with the magic of a game that made him forget hunger and pain, insult and injury.

It was thus, at the age of eleven that he was spotted by one of the members of the Brazilian football team— Valdemar de Brito. This World Cup footballer incredulously watched the sight of this boy playing with his friends. He couldn't believe what he was seeing.

In order to earn money, the teenaged Pelé began playing locally with the Bauru Athletic Club. This was a local minor-league club, and Pelé had already begun to earn himself a local reputation, when de Brito took him, at the age of sixteen, to Sao Paulo. Here he introduced him to the directors of Santos, a mid-level club team on the coast of Brazil, with the famous words, 'This boy will be the greatest soccer player in the world!'

The disbelieving directors had their first taste of Pelé's genius when, on his first appearance for Santos against Corinthians F.C., he scored a goal right away. At this time, he was only sixteen.

Pelé's greatest moments were to come as a match-winning player for his country. In 1958, people turned on the television to watch the football World Cup being telecast live for the very first time. A skinny seventeen-year-old flickered across black and white screens, running circles around seasoned veterans of the game. By the time that World Cup in Sweden ended, Pelé had become a household name across the world.

As a child prodigy excelling at the very highest levels of the game, Pelé has been a source of inspiration for millions. In the light of his role in Brazil's World Cup victory, Brazilian playwright Nelson Rodrigues anointed Pelé 'the King'. A leading journalist Joao Luiz de Albuquerque wrote about why Pelé's emergence as a great footballer was so special. 'He was the light at the end of the tunnel. All the poor said, "Hey, this guy made it, I can make it." He brought the rest of Brazil with him.'

Amazingly, while Pelé was always voted as the greatest footballer ever, his one regret was not being able to equal his father's record of scoring five goals with headers in one single game! He classed the goal he scored with a brilliant header in the 1970 World Cup final against Italy at Mexico as his best goal. This was also very special because it was Brazil's hundredth World Cup goal.

Considering the rough and tough childhood Pelé had to live through, due to poverty and deprivation, it is extremely creditable that he later went on to campaign for children.

On October 1, 1977, Pelé played his last match, an exhibition game between Cosmos, the New York club he played for in the US, and Santos, his former club. Speaking before the game to a worldwide audience, Pelé urged the people to pay attention to the children of the world. He played the first half of that match for Cosmos, and the second half for Santos. A sad and sorrowful audience at the Giants stadium bid this football genius farewell. The skies were leaden and grey, leading a Brazilian newspaper to remark in headlines about that rainy day, 'Even the Sky Was Crying'.

Pelé spent twenty-two years of his life playing soccer, which he called 'the beautiful game', and contributed hugely to international goodwill and friendship, even as he inspired the poorest and most disadvantaged people in his country and elsewhere.

Steven Spielberg

(b. 1946)

Best known as the director of *Jurassic Park*, Steven Spielberg has directed many of the most successful films in Hollywood history, including *Jaws* (1975), *ET* (1982), *Close Encounters of the Third Kind* (1977), *Raiders of the Lost Ark* (1981, co-produced with George Lucas) and *War of the Worlds* (2005). Apart from being known for these hits that combine a strong science fiction element with some good old-fashioned suspense and storytelling, Spielberg has also made more serious films such as *The Color Purple* (1985), *Schindler's List* (1993) and *Saving Private Ryan* (1998). Spielberg founded the studio Dreamworks SKG in 1994, with two other well-known Hollywood directors, Jeffrey Katzenberg and David Geffen. He won Oscars for best director and best picture for *Schindler's List* in 1994. He also won an Oscar for best director for *Saving Private Ryan* and was given the Academy's Irving G. Thalberg Award in 1987 for his contributions to the industry. Spielberg is married to actress Kate Capshaw since 1991. He was earlier married to actress Amy Irving, with whom he has a son. He lives with Kate and their five children in Los Angeles, close to the ocean.

'That pilot from the war whose story I was telling you yesterday, his body's right here, rotting in the upstairs closet!' said the boy, with shining, earnest eyes. 'I saw him when I went to search for my Scout badge in the back. Want to see him?'

His three younger sisters stared back at Steven. They never knew what to expect, with him around. Just the day before, he had told them the sad tale of a World War II hero, who had been one of the most adventurous aviators and lived in the very house they lived in. This time it looked as if he was telling the truth. But what if this was to be just another scenario from his vivid imagination? Should they risk looking? Under the spell of his persuasive talk, his completely serious manner, they went upstairs to the closet used to store out-of-season clothes and footwear.

Anne parted the long coats and woollen scarves. 'What are you talking about?' she asked. 'There doesn't seem to be anything.' Nancy and Sue, who were shorter, started back in alarm. 'Didn't you see?' they hissed at her. 'He's lying in the back!'

'I want to go tell M-m-m-a-m-a ...' said the youngest, her teeth beginning to chatter, as she imagined the corpse in the closet.

'First take a good look and tell me if he's real!' said Steven, gently pushing her towards the other two. When all three had stepped inside the big closet, he stepped back and closed the door. Then he quickly put on a switch at the end of a long wire that was connected to a plastic skull inside the closet. The skull glowed with an eerie light and the sisters, too terrified to notice that the World War II aviator cap and goggles on the head belonged to their father, screamed inside the dark space.

'What's the matter?' said a grinning Steven, opening the door. 'Haven't you ever seen those goggles before?' His shaken sisters did not know whether to fight with Steven for having fooled them so completely, or admire his ingenuity in designing such a truly good scare. That was often the way it was with them. Later, in recalling his childhood, he once said, 'It's amazing that they didn't kill me when we were growing up.'

Steven Spielberg was born on December 18, 1946, in Cincinnati, the eldest child of Arnold and Leahanni Spielberg. His father was a computer engineer, and his mother was a concert pianist. In his childhood, the family moved frequently, living in different towns in New Jersey and Arizona. When his parents divorced, Steven's sisters continued to live in Arizona with his mother, while he moved to what is now Silicon Valley in California, with his father.

Steven was an impressionable child, on whom things he saw on TV made a great impression. He once cried for hours after seeing a documentary on snakes. His first big-theatre movie experience was Cecil B. DeMille's *The Greatest Show on Earth* in 1952, when he was a mere six years old. This film, made on a grand scale about life in the circus, captivated Steven and opened his eyes to a world of imagination, with which he would produce his own images on screen.

His active imagination had full play during his growing up years. He was a thin, sensitive child, who was not too good at sports, and preferred to spend much of his time alone in his bedroom with the door closed. Here even the grotesque shadows of trees outside his window and the cracks in the wall fed his imagination to make up stories that were invariably tinged with a scary element.

Steven began to savour the thrill of being scared quite early. He recalled as an adult, 'As a kid I liked pushing myself to the brink of terror and then pulling back.'

When the family was living in Phoenix, Arizona, Steven was designated the official cameraman of the family, since his father was not very good with a camera. This meant that the boy directed his family members in shooting all their home movies, much in the manner of his adult years, when he would be giving directions to leading actors and technicians on multi-million dollar sets.

He could not get good grades in school, because he was poor in mathematics, and refused to apply himself. However, he was a positive genius in rigging up all manner of gadgets and gimmicks—like the device that had scared his sisters in the closet—using inventive skills inherited from his engineer father. His lack of application in school haunted him later, when he applied for admission to the UCLA School of Theater, Film and Television and University of Southern California's School of Cinema-Television three times but was refused admission due to his poor school grades. He finally obtained his degree in film-making in 2002, thirty-five years after beginning college and studying English at the California State College at Long Beach. Spielberg finished his degree by submitting independent projects at the California State University Long Beach campus, and was awarded a B.A. in film production and electronic arts with an option in film/video production. By this time, he had become a household name as a film director in many parts of the world!

One of the earliest traits that Steven Spielberg showed as a boy was his concern for the less fortunate. Steven would make amateur films with an 8 mm camera and show them to a neighbourhood audience, charging for admission, while his sister sold popcorn. But the proceeds from these screenings would be given to a local school for the handicapped. His whole family enthusiastically supported him in these efforts, which is the reason why he was able to build whole stories on film even as a teenager.

Different subjects captured his imagination in those early experiments with the visual medium. For his merit badge as a Boy Scout, he shot a three-minute film called *Gunsmog* inspired by a TV cowboy show. He shot it in the desert near his home, with fellow scouts playing various roles. The action included a stagecoach holdup, and a villain plunging off a cliff that was actually a dummy made with pillows and shoes.

Even in these boyish films, Spielberg had understood the craft of film-making to a degree far beyond his years. He set up shots with different angles and used primitive special effects in his films. At the age of thirteen, he made a film called *Escape to Nowhere* which was forty minutes long and had a war as its subject. Increasingly complex and ambitious films were to come out of his teen years. At sixteen, he filmed a feature-length science fiction film called *Firelight*. This 140-minute-long film had a complex plot involving astronomers, eerie lights in the evening sky, and a rather violent encounter with some aliens—all themes that would repeat themselves in blockbusters like *ET* and *Close Encounters of the Third Kind*.

Steven Spielberg credits his success as a film-maker to his not having forgotten what it means to be a child, having retained all the wonder and excitement of a child's imagination. Truly, those magical images he dreamed up alone in his bedroom as a child have gone on to enchant and entertain millions of children and grown-ups all over the world.

Mark Spitz

(b. 1950)

The 1972 Olympics at Munich will always be remembered for two things—Mark Spitz winning an astounding seven gold medals in swimming, with every win a record-breaking one, and the murder of eleven Israeli athletes by terrorists. While terrorism has continued with its own ugly history, Mark Spitz continues to be the inspiration for young swimmers fired with the passion to compete and excel. Born on February 10, 1950, Mark Spitz set twenty-three world records and thirty-five US records in swimming. Apart from his all-time record of four individual and three relay gold medals in the 1972 Olympics, he also won two gold, one silver, and one bronze medal in the 1968 Olympics at Mexico. His athletic prowess and drive to win were second to none.

The outings to Waikiki beach in Hawaii were supposed to be fun for the small family of Lenore and Arnold Spitz. Arnold, a steel company executive who had been posted to Honolulu, saw the beach as a place to relax with his wife and two children. But he was unprepared for the reaction of his eldest son Mark, then two years old, to the water. The little boy hurled himself upon the waves with such enjoyment, that his parents were amazed. It seemed as if he was embracing a long-lost friend.

Noting his son's extraordinary love for swimming, Arnold Spitz began taking him to swim at Waikiki every day. Years later, after Mark Spitz had become America's most famous swimmer, his mother declared in an interview to *Time* magazine, 'You should have seen that little boy dash into the ocean. He'd run like he was trying to commit suicide.' For father and son, four years of swimming together in Hawaii passed quickly, till the family moved to California.

Here six-year-old Mark began swimming regularly at the YMCA. His father, sensing a keenly competitive instinct in his son, repeatedly reminded him, 'Swimming isn't everything, winning is.' From his earliest moments, Mark was set to prove he was the best and the fastest, and this made him stand out from his competition wherever he participated. When he was nine years old, he began training under the renowned swimming coach Sherm Chavoor at Arden Hills Swim Club.

Mark Spitz was born Jewish, and when he was ten, his afternoon swimming lessons began to clash with lessons in Hebrew, the language of the Jewish scriptures. In an effort to convince the rabbi (Jewish priest) that his son should be permitted to miss the Hebrew class and continue swimming, Arnold Spitz told him, 'Even God likes a winner.' And it seemed as if Mark really had some divine help when he held seventeen national age-group world records by the time he was ten years old. He was named the world's best ten-and-under swimmer.

The family moved to Santa Clara by the time he was fourteen, so that Mark would be able to train with George Haines of the Santa Clara Swim Club. From this new location, Mark's father commuted more than eighty miles to work every day, but thought it well worth the sacrifice. He was convinced that his son was set to be a swimming great, and had decided it was 'now or never'.

So much stress on winning and competing did not come without its side effects. By the time Mark was seventeen years old in 1967, he had won five gold medals at the Pan-American Games in Winnipeg. At this stage in his life, he held ten world records. By his eighteenth year, he had won twenty-six national and international titles and broken twenty-six US records along with the ten world records. When the 1968 Olympics came around, Mark Spitz had come to believe he was completely unbeatable, and had no hesitation in saying so. He announced to the public that he would win six gold medals at the Olympics.

Such a rash and premature declaration, that too by a mere eighteen-year-old, seemed to smack of arrogance, and many wondered at it. In fact, a humbling experience was due for Mark in Mexico. By making such public promises, Mark Spitz had put an enormous amount of pressure on himself. Even though he won a silver and a bronze medal in individual events and a gold in the team events, it was not enough to silence the critics who had thought him brash and over-confident. For a lesser competitor or athlete, this level of achievement may have been enough, but not for Mark Spitz.

He came back from the disappointment of Mexico and enrolled at Indiana University, where he immediately entered the pool under the expert and watchful eyes of Doc Counselman, the third and last of his famous coaches. Mark performed brilliantly under Counselman, building an awesome college career at Indiana where he continued to win at every event he swam. Spitz led Counselman's team to four national Amateur Athletic Union Championships, where he won eight individual NCAA titles. In his second year at college, he won the Sullivan Award, given to the top amateur athlete in the US. He was named the World Swimmer of the Year all three years he was at college. All this was fine preparation for the Olympics of 1972—the pinnacle of his career.

Four years after his cocky declarations about Olympic medals, Mark Spitz was a changed and mature individual. The twenty-two-year-old was hounded by reporters everywhere he went, all asking, 'How many medals?' But he just refused to give in. At the time, he represented an oddity in sport—he was the only swimmer to be sporting a moustache! This also attracted its fair share of attention, with people lavishing praise on his looks and his moustache. All great athletes and famous personalities have to learn to live with such distractions. The wisest of them do not let such considerations get in the way of their performance.

At Munich in 1972, Spitz won his first gold medal in the 200-metre butterfly in two minutes and seven-tenths of a second, for a world record, on August 28. Later that same night, his second gold medal came when his team set a world record for the 400-metre free-style relay The following day, he won his third gold medal, this time establishing a world record when he swam the 200-metre free-style in one minute and 52.78 seconds. On September 1, he swam the 100-metre butterfly in 54.27 seconds to earn a world record and another gold medal. He was the anchor for the US 800-metre free-style relay team in their victory for another gold medal. He won the 100-metre free-style in 51.22 seconds and swam the butterfly leg on the victorious US team in the 400-metre medley relay for his seventh gold medal on September 3. When Mark Spitz won seven gold medals at a single Olympic Games, he was surpassing another world record—the one held by Italian fencer Nedo Nadi, who had won five Olympic gold medals in 1920.

The tragic events that unfolded in the next few days, with the killing of eleven Israeli athletes, cast a cloud over Mark's achievements for a while. Himself a Jew, he had to be escorted back home under heavy security and could not savour his victory as much as he would have wanted to. However, what he had achieved was going to stand the test of time for a very long time. In recent years, Australian swimmer Ian Thorpe with five gold medals at the Olympics, and US swimmer Michael Phelps, with six, have been the only ones to come close enough to be considered anywhere as good as Spitz.

After his triumphant Olympics showing, Mark Spitz came back to some television and speaking assignments, and advertising endorsements, before settling down to a career in real estate. He enjoyed spending time with his family, wife Suzy and sons, Matt and Justin. He nearly returned to the world swimming stage at the ripe age of forty-one, after going into training at thirty-nine!

Mark Spitz is a sporting legend whose words have inspired many. One of his most memorable quotes is, 'If you fail to prepare, you're prepared to fail.' Recounting his own reactions to his success, Mark observed, 'Did I take it all in on the awards stand? The only time I would have done that was my last event, because I was always thinking about the next one.'

Being truly focused on the next race, and the next race alone, is one of the hallmarks of a winner like Mark Spitz.

Kapil Dev

(b. 1959)

Kapil Dev played cricket for India and Haryana, besides Northamptonshire and Worcestershire in English county cricket. He is widely regarded as one of the greatest all-round cricketers of all time. A right-arm, fast-medium bowler, and a forceful middle-order batsman who hit the ball with tremendous power, he made his Test debut at the tender age of nineteen in 1978 against Pakistan at Faisalabad. He was captain of the Indian team in thirty-four Tests, out of which India managed to win only four. However, his most memorable feat is leading India to victory in the 1983 World Cup final against the then-reigning cricket super power West Indies. When Kapil retired from cricket in 1994 he had played in 131 Tests, taken a record 434 Test wickets and scored 5,248 runs at an average of 31.05, with eight centuries and twenty-seven half-centuries. Kapil Dev had competition from the likes of Ian Botham, Imran Khan and Richard Hadlee for the position of the best all-rounder in the world during the 1980s. Most people saw Kapil as a people's champion, a symbol of the hopes and aspirations of millions of Indians. He took five wickets or more in a Test innings twenty-three times during his career. His most memorable knock was during the 1983 World Cup in England. India were on the verge of defeat to Zimbabwe and he went on

177

to ensure India's victory by scoring 175 not out with sixteen fours and six sixes. It was after this great performance by Kapil that India went on to win the finals. Since his retirement, Kapil Dev has been involved in cricket administration and broadcasting. He launched the Indian Cricket League in 2007.

———————————

A slight sound in his garden woke up the gentleman from his Sunday afternoon nap. Hurrying to open the door to his balcony, he was just in time to see the last of the group of small boys scramble over the wall and run away to the next compound.

'Hey!' he yelled, peering at the young figures. He thought he recognised one particular silhouette. It was the young Nikhanj boy, encouraging his friends to steal guavas. 'Hey!' yelled the man again. Then he leaned over the edge of his balcony and shouted, 'I have seen you Kapil, don't think you're getting away with this! Your father will know very soon that you've been stealing the neighbour's guavas again!'

The only sign that his threat had been heard was a

grin flashed at him from the safe distance of the nearby compound in the Chandigarh colony. It was an afternoon like many others for the young and mischievous Kapil Dev.

Kapil Dev was born on January 6, 1959, in Chandigarh, the sixth child of Ram Lal Nikhanj and his wife Raj Kumari Lajwanti. During the Partition, Kapil's parents had arrived in Chandigarh from a village near Rawalpindi. In Chandigarh, Ram Lal Nikhanj set up a construction and timber business. Kapil Dev went to D.A.V. School and was like any other child in his neighbourhood—feisty, fun-loving and mad about sports.

This bunch of 'crazy kids' as Kapil describes the friends of his childhood, played cricket on the streets and on any available ground. Kapil's school did not have a cricket ground in those days. Chandigarh was not the large city it is today—it was more like a sprawling town, and the children had ample opportunity to spend hours playing their favourite games. Kapil's initial experience of cricket was hardly orthodox or well-organised. As he recalled at a public function recently, 'We played with anything we could lay our hands on—hockey sticks, flat sticks and the all-time favourite, the broad *thappi* used for washing clothes. Marbles and kite-flying were my other passions.'

It was inevitable that so much time spent dreaming of and playing sports meant that Kapil gave no more than a passing attention to his studies! But at age thirteen, an opportunity opened for him to be known at a higher level than school-level games. Kapil was asked to play in a local league match when one of the Chandigarh sector teams was a player short. He showed such talent at this level, that he began to be called for matches again and again. Kapil was finally being noticed at the state level. His debut for the Indian team came at the comparatively young age of nineteen.

In October 1978, a shock-haired young bowler sent fearsomely fast deliveries to the Pakistan side and captured the imagination of the entire subcontinent. Both India and Pakistan watched the teenager in action at Faisalabad, and it was obvious that a new star had appeared on the horizon of Indian cricket. What was remarkable was that Kapil Dev came from comparatively obscure origins into what till then had been perceived as a 'gentleman's game' largely played by boys from the big cities.

In fact, Kapil himself believes that the smaller towns are ideal for grooming young sportsmen because children do not have to waste time commuting—from their school to home to tuition classes. The time saved could be devoted to sports. It is also true that Kapil brought an edge to competitive cricket because of his hunger for the game itself, something that people who grow up in a more privileged environment sometimes lack. He also showed a very high degree of self-motivation in grooming himself into a cricketer of international repute. His family recalled that as a boy, he was more effective than any alarm clock in getting them to jump out of bed! His mother also praised his uncomplaining nature as a child in a large family, with many siblings. 'I never even spent a single rupee on his career, he did it all by himself. Since his childhood, he was never the one to bother about food or clothes; it was only cricket that mattered to him,' said his mother in 2002, when Kapil was declared the Wisden Indian cricketer of the century.

As a boy, Kapil followed the fortunes of the Indian cricket team with great passion. While his father encouraged him to play, and was his first role model, his elder brother was also an inspiration. Later Kapil idolised G.R. Viswanath, one of India's greatest batsmen ever, who was in fine form in the 1970s. Viswanath scored fourteen Test centuries, and in every match that he scored thus, India either won or drew the match. A great team man, and one who epitomised the spontaneous, courageous and emotional aspect of batting and playing, Viswanath was indeed a fitting role model for Kapil, who later went on to become the sole reason for India getting a berth in the 1983 cricket World Cup final.

Kapil began playing for Haryana at the age of sixteen, making his debut in a match against Punjab in the Ranji Trophy in 1975-76, when he took 6 for 39 in the first innings. He began the match as a spinner, then changed to fast swing bowling. His first-class career is also populated with brilliant records. He has made

10,800 runs, including sixteen centuries, and taken 815 wickets in first-class cricket.

Kapil's records have been tested by other cricketers after him, but they are still remarkable as a testament to his fighting spirit in life and cricket. He used to run the distance of 46 km between Ambala and Chandigarh to remain at the peak of physical fitness. He completed the 'double' of 1000 runs and 100 wickets in Test cricket when he was just twenty-one, and was the youngest player to complete 2000 runs and 200 wickets in Test cricket when he was twenty-four. He was not known as the 'Haryana Hurricane' for nothing, and has been an immensely popular personality on and off the field.

J.K. Rowling

(b. 1965)

J.K. Rowling is the pen name of Joanne Rowling, a British writer known throughout the world as the author of the Harry Potter series of books. The Potter books speak of a parallel world to our own where there is witchcraft and magic, and where a young boy goes to the Hogwarts School of Magic to learn to become a wizard. They have been the most popular books of recent times, winning multiple awards, and selling millions of copies in sixty-three languages. For the publishing industry, Harry Potter has been the best news in decades. The last four Potter books were consecutively the fastest-selling books in history. J.K. Rowling's work brought children back to reading and storytelling at a time when computers, the internet, and video games were seen to be destroying many aspects of childhood. Harry Potter is now a global brand which has led to J.K. Rowling becoming one of the richest people in the world. While the direction of Rowling's work after the completion of the Harry Potter series is not immediately evident, she has become a notable philanthropist, supporting several causes and charities. To millions of children and adults worldwide, completely entranced by the antics of Harry Potter, J.K. Rowling is an unforgettable contemporary icon.

'Please, please, don't let me fall to my death,' pleaded the dark-haired girl. 'Just hold on tight and let me climb back up.'

'What will you give me if I hold on?' asked her fair-haired sister, whose face could just be seen between the banisters while her arms protruded from both sides, holding on to the sister who swung by her arms over the steep drop of the staircase of their home.

'I will ... I've already promised to give you my velvet-covered notebook and the pen knife Papa gave me for Christmas, you idiot!' said the dark-haired girl. 'Please don't let me go! I'll fa-a-a-all!'

This last was said in such a theatrical wail that it brought their mother running to the spot from the garden where she had been peacefully reading in the shade of a tree.

'Joanne!' said their mother sharply. 'How many times have I told you not to play that awfully silly game? Don't you realise how dangerous it can be?'

Even as the first syllables of her name were leaving her mother's lips, the girl between the banisters had let go of her sister's arms. Her sister fell, landing on her feet—the manner of her fall showing just how often both girls played their favourite 'cliffhanger' game. The girls scurried to make themselves invisible from their visibly cross mother. They knew she was dreadfully angry—why else would she have called Jo by her full name, Joanne?

Joanne was born on July 31, 1965, in a small town

called Yate in Gloucestershire, England, ten miles from Bristol. Her father, Peter James Rowling, and her mother, Anne Rowling, had both worked in the Royal Navy before settling down near Bristol. Joanne was always called Jo by her parents and family, and was just short of her second birthday when her sister Dianne, who was always called Di, was born. The sisters were thus not only close in age, they were also extremely close in childhood—either fighting 'like a pair of wildcats imprisoned together in a very small cage' as J.K. Rowling has described it, or sharing games and stories, friends and daring escapades.

As a baby, Jo was plump, and later grew to have freckles. She was also somewhat short-sighted, quiet and not good at sports. These were perhaps the factors that led to her being labelled the 'bright' one in the family, while Di, who had dark hair and eyes like her mother, was considered the 'pretty' one. Both the girls resented their labels, considering them unjustified and limiting, but as family traditions are wont to do, they stayed, at least during the years both of them were growing up. Jo and Di spent a good part of their time together fighting, sometimes with dire results. Once, Jo threw a battery at her sister, causing her to get a cut above her eye. Jo's defence to her enraged mother was, 'I didn't think I would actually hit her! I thought she would duck!' Understandably, her mother was not impressed by this excuse.

From the age of around three to the time she was

nine, Joanne lived in Winterbourne, on the outskirts of Bristol. This was the house with stairs where she and her sister so loved to play their cliff game again and again. Here she went to a school that provided plenty of scope for crafts and creativity. As she recalls, 'I enjoyed school in Winterbourne. It was a very relaxed environment; I remember lots of pottery- making, drawing and story-writing, which suited me perfectly.' Very fond of making up stories to tell her sister, Joanne wrote her first 'book' at the age of six. This was called 'Rabbit' and featured a rabbit which gets sick with the measles and is visited by his friends, including a giant bee called Miss Bee!

Around the time she was seven, Jo and her sister were friends with a brother and sister named Potter who lived on their street. This surname was later to be immortalised as Harry Potter's last name. While the real person, Ian Potter, who was Joanne's neighbour, bears no resemblance to Harry's character, there are other figures from her childhood who are said to inhabit her books, among them her elderly headmaster at St Michaels Primary School, Alfred Dunn, who turns up in the Harry Potter books as Albus Dumbledore.

Jo and Di's parents had always dreamt of living in the country, and around Joanne's ninth birthday the family moved to Tutshill, a small village just outside Chepstow, in Wales. It was around this time that Joanne lost a favourite grandparent, her paternal grandmother, Kathleen. Later in life, when her publishers felt that a book about a boy would not be appreciated by boy readers if it was by a female author, Joanne added the initial 'K' to her name in honour of this grandmother, so that her name, J.K. Rowling could be interpreted either as a man or woman writer.

Distressed by the loss of her grandmother, Joanne did not settle well into her new school that had old-fashioned roll-top desks facing the blackboard. Her most enduring memories of this school are the hours she spent enlarging a hole that had been gouged into the desk by the boy who had sat there before her, with the point of her compass. She worked diligently on the hole 'so that by the time I left that classroom you could comfortably wiggle your thumb through it.'

Better times were to come when Joanne moved to her secondary school called Wyedean, when she was eleven. Here she made firm friends with Sean Harris, who owned a turquoise-and-white Ford Anglia. Zooming off into the darkness in Sean's car spelt a great deal of freedom to Joanne, since life in the countryside meant that transport was erratic and she often had to ask her father for a lift to wherever she wanted to go. Sean was special not only for being the first of Joanne's friends who learnt to drive a car, but also because he was the first person with whom she discussed her serious ambition to be a writer. He sincerely felt that Joanne would be a great success at it, and this meant a lot to her. She later dedicated the second Potter book, *The Chamber of Secrets* to Sean, and his car also features as the magic vehicle that takes Ron and Harry crashing into the Whomping Willow and finally disappears into the Enchanted Forest.

The darker themes of sadness and loss, particularly of Harry's own parents, in Joanne's books, undoubtedly have a lot to do with the fact that her mother was diagnosed with multiple sclerosis (MS), a crippling and degenerative disease of the central nervous system, when she was fifteen. Although it is possible for many people with MS to pursue a near-normal life with care, Joanne's mother's illness grew steadily worse after her diagnosis, and this cast a shadow over the whole family during her teenage years.

From her carefree roughhousing with her sister, to the deeper realisations brought about by her mother's illness and subsequent passing away, J.K. Rowling has captured a whole spectrum of action and emotion that particularly appeals to contemporary young readers.

A.R. Rahman

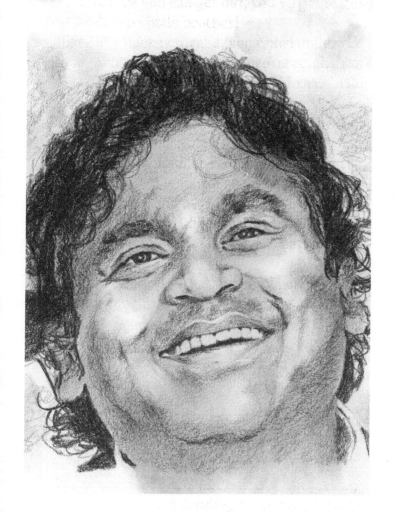

(b. 1967)

No other composer or music director from India has received as much attention in recent times as A.R. Rahman. He has redefined contemporary Indian music by bringing together elements from folk, classical and pop music from all over the world in a way that millions of listeners find truly mesmerising. A.R. Rahman has not only demolished all the conventional rules in music, he has also transcended geographical boundaries with the sheer popularity of his songs. His music has been a hit in every corner of India, and he is a respected name on the international scene as well, having worked with musicians like Nusrat Fateh Ali Khan, Michael Jackson, Sir Andrew Lloyd Webber, Deep Forest, Apache Indian, Zakir Hussain, L. Shankar, David Byrne, Kadri Gopalnath, Vikku Vinayakram, Ustad Sultan Khan, Pandit Vishwa Mohan Bhatt and many others. With Rahman, the music of South Indian cinema began to be appreciated on a national scale, and the cassettes and CDs of many films sold better and were more popular than the films themselves. Rahman has a perfect sense of melody and rhythm and is a wonderfully talented sound engineer, completely at home with the technology of the digital age. While he has been accused of everything from repetition to burnout, his music continues to enjoy unrivalled popularity. He lives and works in Chennai, and predominantly composes for Tamil cinema after having composed for Hindi films, international theatre, and original albums with international artistes. The songs he sung himself have been particularly well-received, and he is also known as a music director who has introduced many fresh new voices to playback singing.

By the time the music director had finally recorded the song to his satisfaction, it was nearly 10 pm. The singer was the first to leave the studio. Soon other members of the orchestra began to put away their instruments and get ready to leave too. They all looked tired. But unlike the others, there was one member of the orchestra who was not thinking of the family that awaited him, or of the responsibilities that shaped his adult life. The head of this keyboard player was instead buzzing with tunes. As he covered his instrument, the tune he had just played joined many others in his head.

'Come on Dileep, your mother must be waiting. Murugesan is lingering only to give you a lift home,' called one of his colleagues in the orchestra.

'Coming, anna (elder brother),' said the keyboard player, as he moved out of the recording studio. His colleague gave him an encouraging pat on his head as farewell.

The keyboard player was eleven years old.

A.R. Rahman was born A.S. Dileep Kumar on January 6, 1967 in Chennai to R.K. Sekhar and Kasthuri. His father was a composer who worked as an orchestra arranger and conductor in Malayalam films. Dileep was the only son. He has an elder sister, Kanchana, and two younger sisters, now called Talath and Israth. His mother later became Kareema Begum. Dileep often accompanied his father to the studio and liked being surrounded by musical instruments and the paraphernalia of recording. He was discovered playing a tune on the harmonium when he was all of four years old! What was even more remarkable was that the person who found him at it, a music director called Sudarshanam Master, had covered the harmonium keys with a cloth. But this made no difference to the four-year-old, who replayed the tune effortlessly! 'This boy must receive training in music,' declared the music director. Perhaps this was one of the reasons Dileep started learning the piano at the age of four from Dhanraj Master.

More than music, which came so naturally to him,

little Dileep was fascinated by computers and engineering. In fact, he wanted to be a computer engineer when he grew up. This fascination with technology emerged very strongly when his father bought a synthesiser, one of the earliest in Chennai to do so, from Singapore. Drawn irresistibly to this forbidden toy, Dileep spent hours experimenting with its varied notes and sounds. These were the happier memories of his childhood.

Unfortunately, all this was to be overturned only too soon, with the tragic passing away of his father on the same day that Sekhar's first film as a composer was released. Dileep was then just nine years old. Not only did he have to struggle with his own grief at the loss of a beloved parent, he also had to deal with rumours about his father's death in the deeply superstitious world of the film industry. All of this severely tested his faith in God. It was rumoured that his father had been done in by black magic, due to work-related rivalries. Dileep had to witness his mother's abject prayers go unanswered, through his father's illness and ultimate death.

After this life-altering event, for a time the family supported itself by lending out the father's musical instruments. Then, when he turned eleven, Dileep joined the famous music director Ilayaraja's troupe as a keyboard player in order to earn money for his family. He began to play the guitar, too, and played the keyboard for some programmes on television.

But this work deprived Dileep of the time and space needed to complete his school education. After being forced to move out of a well-known school for low attendance, he struggled at another, before dropping out of school altogether in Class XI.

But Dileep had little or no regrets. What could be better than playing in the orchestra of M.S. Vishwanathan, and accompanying Zakir Hussain and violinist Kunnakudi Vaidyanathan on world tours? He was also seen playing the keyboard on the popular music TV show *Wonder Balloon* on Madras Doordarshan. He began making short forays into music composition for films under Ilayaraja, such as the theme music for one of K. Balachander's films.

While working with Ilaiyaraja, the young and impressionable boy learnt an important lesson. As he describes it, 'Until then I thought you had to drink or take dope to be a good artist. But Ilayaraja was making such beautiful music and leading a pure life!' Earlier exposed to the stereotype of musicians taking alcohol or drugs to make their music, he saw from Ilayaraja's example for the first time how music was a discipline, a way of life all its own. The lesson was an enduring one. He recalls, 'He proved that he could make good music without any bad habits! Even now he is an inspiration for me being so religious today.'

Fortunately for him, Dileep earned a scholarship to the famed Trinity College of Music and completed a degree in Western classical music. When he returned, he was fired with the desire to bring an international and contemporary world perspective to Indian music. He played with local rock bands like Roots, Magic and Nemesis Avenue with friends and future colleagues like Suresh Peters, Ranjit Barot and Sivamani Anandan. This continued till he began making a living as a composer of advertising jingles. It was this departure that led to his discovery by Maniratnam for the soundtrack of *Roja* in 1991. And the amazingly successful career that followed thereafter.

But before this discovery, the second and most significant of the events that shaped his life had occurred. When his sister was seriously ill in 1988, all attempts to cure her failed and it appeared the family was heading for another tragedy. At this time, a Muslim pir Sheik Abdul Qadir Jeelani helped his sister to make a miraculous recovery. Deeply influenced by this experience, the family converted to Islam, and A.S. Dileep Kumar became Allah Rakha Rahman.

A very religious and devout Muslim, Rahman's music is an expression of his profound faith. He describes his journey thus, 'After my father passed away, for some years, when I was a teenager, I believed there was no God. But there was a feeling of restlessness within me. I realised that there can be no life without a force governing us ... without one God. And I found what I was looking for in Islam.' As for his views on what makes a great musician or artiste, 'Personally, I would say that a sense of spirituality helps a great deal. And it is important that you study life as well. Both these things will make a better human being, and therefore, a better composer out of you. Life teaches you what real pain and happiness are, and these things help in creating better compositions. It works like this: if the film demands happy music the composer only has to tap into the wellspring of happy experiences from his own life to create the right ambience for that tune. I think this is more important than learning all the technical gymnastics of music.'

The man who has mastered technology for musical expression is still driven by the engine of faith in life and God.

Brian Lara

(b. 1969)

Brian Lara (born May 2, 1969) has been one of the most prolific batsmen in modern-day cricket. Lara regularly created records that may stand forever in the record books. A native of Trinidad and Tobago, he has captained West Indies three times, from 1997 to 1999, from 2003 to 2004, and in his last stint, from April 2006 to April 2007. He announced his retirement from international cricket during the cricket World Cup, and played his last match against England on April 21, 2007. Millions of fans worldwide bade him an emotional farewell on that day, remembering the batting feats that have made him hold the record for the highest individual innings and as the all-time leading run scorer in Test cricket, scoring 400 runs in a single innings against England in 2004. He also holds the record for the highest individual score in first class cricket, with a total of 501 not out for Warwickshire against Durham at Edgbaston in 1994.

Agnes Cyrus was returning home at dusk one evening in the small town of Cantaro in Trinidad and Tobago when she saw a poster announcing the Harvard coaching clinic for cricket. 'Training in the best batting techniques by batsmen with impeccable credentials' it read. The weekly clinic invited young cricketers who wanted to make a mark in the game.

Agnes did not play cricket, but as soon as she saw the poster, the image of her second-youngest brother, Brian sprung to her mind. It was the year 1975. This boy, then all of six years old, had taken a bat in his hand at the age of three, and seemed to have rarely parted from it since. The tenth child in a family of eleven children in the home of Bunty and Pearl Lara, Brian was never short of siblings who were ready to bowl to him, as he batted the ball to astonishing distances, far beyond the yard of their modest home. Agnes wanted Brian to enroll at the Harvard cricket clinic.

As soon as she reached home, she excitedly broke the news about the coaching clinic to her father, sitting on the porch of their house in the gathering dark. 'It would be just the thing for Brian, Papa!' she exclaimed. 'You know, he was born to bat!' Bunty Lara stroked the stubble on his chin thoughtfully. His wife was chopping beans and cabbage for dinner. 'Yes, that he decidedly is,' he said. 'I will see what I can do.'

Even though the family's resources were often stretched to the limit, with thirteen members, eleven of them growing children, Bunty Lara was determined to fuel the spark of pure genius he had noticed in his son Brian, from a very early age.

Brian used to accompany his father to the big cricket

matches whenever they were held at nearby venues. When he was five years old, he saw Colin Cowdrey bat for England. Brian was so mesmerised by the sight that he came home and asked his brothers, his father and godfather to bowl to him over several days till he was satisfied that he had hit each of the strokes he had seen Cowdrey play! Cowdrey remained his idol till he saw Roy Fredericks.

Roy Fredericks proved even more inspiring than Cowdrey, because he was a left-hander like Brian himself. The West Indies opening batsman had a dashing batting style and a distinguished style of dressing that Brian did his best to emulate. He asked his father to buy him a white shirt with long sleeves. Brian wore this shirt, buttoned up at the wrists, whenever he went out to bat against other young boys in the local matches. It was this, and his phenomenally prolific batting, that earned him the nickname Roy Fredericks among his peers.

Bunty Lara enrolled his son at the Harvard coaching clinic, where he learnt batting techniques. For nine long years, every Sunday from January to June, father and son would travel the distance from home to the clinic. Brian made rapid progress and justified his family's faith in his talent. Hugo Day, the coach at Harvard, spotted Brian's exceptional ability almost immediately, and quickly promoted him from batting against tennis balls to real cricket balls, even though he was still so small. When the Harvard clinic team toured neighbouring Barbados, Brian's batting drew the attention of Carlisle Best, a batsman for Barbados and the West Indies. In recognition of his talent, Best gifted Brian a bat.

Brian cherished this bat, which stayed with him till he toured India in 1985 as a member of the Trinidad and Tobago secondary schools team. Other great batsmen were also moved to give a bat to Brian, among them Gus Logie, one of Brian's idols and a leading batsman for Trinidad and Tobago. Such encouragement from his seniors in the sport went a long way in nourishing his spirit.

However, Brian Lara may well have got distracted from his life's mission if his father had not guided him in the right direction on one particular afternoon. All of Brian's elder brothers played both cricket and football. Both the sports appealed equally to Brian too. One Sunday afternoon, Brian wanted to go to St Augustine Senior Comprehensive School, to a trial for the national youth football squad that was to tour Puerto Rico. The same afternoon, Harvard's clinic had scheduled double-wicket and single-wicket competitions. When Brian went to ask his father if he could try for the football selections, Bunty Lara looked him straight in the eye and said, 'Son, if you are going to play cricket, count me in, if you go for the football, count me out!' Such a clear command from a loving and supportive parent convinced Brian that his future lay in cricket, not in football.

From those early moments, Brian Lara's exceptional career was marked with the same focus, determination and drive that have also been seen in his contemporary, Sachin Tendulkar. Besides being contemporaries, Sachin and Brian have also rivalled each other for cricketing records. Brian was so passionate about the game, that he built a whole solitary world around it. He describes it in his autobiography, *Beating the Field*, 'When the others grew tired and went home and there was no one else to play with, I used to play my own Test matches on the porch of our house, using a broom handle or a stick as the bat and a marble as the ball. I would arrange the potted plants to represent fielders and try to find the gaps as I played my shots.'

From this single-minded devotion to the game came a confidence that marked his entire career. When he was touring India as a young schoolboy in 1985, a senior cricket writer asked him what he did and he replied, 'I'm a batsman who tops the batting averages.' A simple statement that stayed true throughout his career in cricket.

In recent years, Brian Lara has been a source of inspiration and encouragement to other young cricketers. Dwayne Bravo, a promising young West Indies cricketer, recalls Brian's advice, which served as a positive reminder to him at many crucial moments: 'You stand at the crossroads of life now and which way you jump depends heavily on you. You can no longer blame bad homes or past failures, because you are old enough to control the workings of your own mind. You can also listen to wise advice. For instance, you are often advised to keep "good" company.

'Why? Because the company you keep influences you in both obvious and subtle ways. Keeping good company means that you can influence each other in positive ways, but when you play with the dogs you get bitten by the fleas!

'Above all, keep the faith. When you put God into the situation, wonderful things take place.'

To millions of his fans, God has really expressed himself through the bat of Brian Lara, taking cricket to dizzying heights that will be difficult to equal in the near future. His love and dedication to the game are a true inspiration for cricketers and cricket lovers the world over.